TEACH
YOUR

CHILD
MATH

Also by Michael Brant Shermer:

Psychling: On Mental and Physical Fitness
Sport Cycling
The Ultra-Marathon Cycling Manual (with John Marino and Lon
   Haldeman)
Cycling: Endurance and Speed
The Woman Cyclist (with Elaine Mariolle)
The RAAM Book (with John Marino and Lon Haldeman)
Teach Your Child Science
Meeting the Challenge of Arthritis (with George Yates)

TEACH YOUR CHILD MATH

MAKING MATH FUN FOR THE BOTH OF YOU

Updated Edition!
Arthur Benjamin, Ph.D.
and
Michael Brant Shermer, Ph.D.
Updated by Ronn Yablun

LOWELL HOUSE
Los Angeles

CONTEMPORARY BOOKS
Chicago

Library of Congress Cataloging-in-Publication Data

Benjamin, Arthur.
    Teach your child math : making math fun for the
both of you / Arthur Benjamin, Michael Brant Shermer.
    p. cm.
  Includes index.
  ISBN 0-929923-32-4
  ISBN 1-56565-481-1 (updated edition)
  1. Mathematics—Study and teaching (Elementary)
2. Education—Parent participation. I. Shermer, Michael. II Title.
QA11.B44   1991
649'.68—dc20   91-3158
                                                         CIP

Requests for such permissions should be addressed to:

LOWELL HOUSE

2020 Avenue of the Stars, Suite 300

Los Angeles, CA 90067

Lowell House books can be purchased at special dis-
counts when ordered in bulk for premiums and special sales. Contact Department TC at the address above.

Design: MIKE YAZZOLINO

Illustrations: BARNEY SALZBERG

Manufactured in the United States of America
10 9 8 7 6 5 4 3 2 1

This book is dedicated to the parents and teachers who have taken the time and effort to teach us both the importance of and the joy to be found in math and science, and to the children who we hope will share in our love of math as a tool to better understand the world around us.

CONTENTS

Acknowledgments   ix

Introduction to the Updated Edition   xi

THE MAGIC OF MATH   1

PART I   Getting Excited About Math

CHAPTER 1.   Every Child as Mathematician   9

CHAPTER 2.   Mathematics as a Game   15

PART II   Let the Games Begin

CHAPTER 3.   Begin at the Beginning: Games of Naming, Sorting, and Comparing   25

CHAPTER 4.   How Many Are There? Games of Ordering, Measuring, and Counting   34

CHAPTER 5.   Summing Up: Addition Games   54

CHAPTER 6.   What's the Difference? Subtraction Games   87

CHAPTER 7.   How Many Times? Multiplication Games   107

CHAPTER 8.   Divide and Conquer: Division Games   129

CHAPTER 9.   Problem Solving: Taking Basic Skills to the Next Level   146

KEEP THE MAGIC IN MATH   163

APPENDICES

APPENDIX 1: Books on Math and Science for Adults   164

APPENDIX 2: Books on Math and Science for Children   169

APPENDIX 3: Math and Science Periodicals for Parents
and Children   171

APPENDIX 4: Math Careers for Your Child   173

APPENDIX 5: Math, Science, and Technology
Museums by Region and State   179

APPENDIX 6: Scientific Companies that Publish Math and
Science Catalogues and Distribute Teaching Tools   189

INDEX   193

Acknowledgments

We would like to acknowledge the valuable editorial feedback from our editor, Janice Gallagher, who helped keep us on track in communicating mathematical ideas in a "user-friendly" manner. Thanks also to Derek Gallagher, Peter Hoffman, and Mary Aarons, who produced the book, as well as to Jack Artenstein for making the project possible.

Introduction to the Updated Edition

The magic of math lies in the ultimate surprise. The surprise is that, in reality, math is extremely useful. Now I'm not trying to put down the other academic areas, but the content of this particular subject does more than just relay information to the student. It applies to many, many aspects of everyday life. You simply cannot go one day without using some form of math. There are very few jobs, if any, that do not use math in one form or another. However, the practical side of the subject is, without question, the most exciting and the most useful.

Once you have taught even the most basic skills to your child, teaching the application aspects of math is even more exciting. Your child will begin to see that he is learning about numbers and operations for a reason. He will begin to see math truly come alive. It opens up a whole new world of possibilities.

Your child will begin to see numbers everywhere—in the grocery store, in the bank, at the post office, and even at home. The reality of math excites a young mind, and the art of teaching math is to bring it to life in a most meaningful way.

Teach Your Child Math was undoubtedly created as a tool to initiate the learning process in math. It is my intent to take this process one step further and help you demonstrate to your child how to apply these basic skills. How can we show your child the significance of numbers and operations in a way that he will begin to see it as real?

In this second edition of *Teach Your Child Math*, we have included a new chapter on problem solving. We begin the chapter with the identification of key words to help children identify the word(s) that will help them solve word problems. We have also added problem-solving situations that use the four basic operations in math: addition, subtraction, multiplication, and division. Now your child will be able to see the reality and purpose of numbers, and mathematics becomes meaningful and real in a way that children can both understand and relate to.

To open a child's eyes to the significance of numbers is to stimulate a child's appetite for knowledge. It is to entice, excite, illuminate, and create a new thirst within the child. This is where it all truly begins.

"Can you do Addition?" the White Queen asked.

"What's one and one and one and one and one and one and one and one and one and one?"

"I don't know," said Alice. "I lost count."

"She can't do Addition," the Red Queen interrupted.

"Can you do Subtraction? Take nine from eight."

"Nine from eight I can't, you know," Alice replied very readily: "but—"

"She can't do Subtraction," said the White Queen. "Can you do Division? Divide a loaf by a knife—what's the answer to *that*?"

"I suppose—" Alice was beginning, but the Red Queen answered for her. "Bread-and-butter, of course. Try another Subtraction sum. Take a bone from a dog: what remains?"

Alice considered. "The bone wouldn't remain, of course, if I took it—and the dog wouldn't remain; it would come to bite me—and I'm sure *I* shouldn't remain!"

—Lewis Carroll, *Through the Looking-Glass*

The Magic of Math

When I* was a child, my favorite toy was a little miniature slot machine. You would press a button and in the four windows would appear an addition, subtraction, multiplication, and division problem. I would try to answer the problem, and then check the answer that appeared in a window above the problem. I loved playing games so much that I mastered that toy, and that's how I learned most of my addition, subtraction, multiplication, and division rules. Math has been a game for me ever since.

In this book we* provide ways of turning math into a game, so that the learning experience is fun for your child. Most parents would like their children to be good at math, but at the same time many adults have a certain fear of math—a math anxiety—which can make teaching children math an uncomfortable and anxiety-producing experience. By making math fun, by turning math *problems* into math *games*, we hope to remove whatever math anxiety you may have, so that both you and your child will learn to love the game the way we do. Herein lies one of the principal reasons we wanted to write this book. The other reasons follow. Briefly, *Teach Your Child Math* will:

---

*All first-person remarks in this book belong to the first author, Dr. Benjamin. "We" refers to both authors.

1

1. *Help you and your child understand both the benefits and the fun to be derived from math.*

A math degree is one of the best degrees you can get as preparation for an M.B.A. (or law degree or medical degree or, in fact, most professional degrees), because you learn *how to solve problems.* Although they are mathematical problems, problem-solving skills learned in one area can be applied to others. If you can understand a proof in advanced algebra or calculus, you will probably be able to understand contract law or anatomy or corporate structure. But even if you just learn basic mathematics, you can still apply the same problem-solving skills to many of the problems you confront in life.

There is a certain basic benefit to your child's having a solid grounding in mathematics upon entering the work force. Jim Pilarski of the Marriott Hotel chain, for example, has noted: "Declining educational standards eliminate some applicants from consideration. We estimate that 30 to 40 percent have limited mathematics and science fundamentals, and that concerns us." Wall Street, business schools, law schools, and medical schools actively pursue students with sharp analytic and reasoning skills.

Your child, of course, isn't concerned with his or her employability a decade or more down the line. Children just want to have fun, but that shouldn't prevent your hidden agenda from having its effect. "The more kids that you get to like mathematics," says Harold Hodgkinson from the Institute for Educational Leadership, "the stronger tomorrow's work force will be."

If you can turn numbers and mathematics into a game for children, they will naturally love to play it. Later, they will understand the benefits derived from playing the game, but in the meantime they're having fun. Numbers are magic, and the games we've designed for you to play with your child will help both of you understand and love math the way Michael and I do. *The secret to successful math education is to make it so much fun that children don't even realize they are learning something that will help them later in life.*

2. *Help stop the decline in math and science education.*

According to a study conducted by the Mathematical Sciences Education Board of the National Research Council, U.S. 8th-grade students were ranked 14th in the world in mathematics, just behind New Zealand and Finland; and while U.S. 12th-grade students fared a little better, they were still ranked 12th in the world in mathematics, behind Scotland and Belgium, countries that hardly spring to mind when one considers worldwide industrial and technological powers. (It comes as no surprise that technologically advanced Japan was 1st and 2nd in these two rankings.)

Our abysmal world ranking is only the beginning. The Committee on the Mathematical Sciences in the Year 2000 reports that "eight of the ten fastest growing jobs will be science-based occupations by 1995," and that "by the year 2000 the U.S. economy is expected to create more than 21 million new jobs, most of which will require both postsecondary education and the use of mathematics" such as "problem-solving ability, and numerical reasoning." At the same time, they report that "unless positive steps are taken now, the nation's needs for mathematically skilled workers will not be met."

We could go on and on with quotes and grim statistics. But the important question is: *Why?* Why are we falling so far behind other, supposedly less advanced countries in the areas of math and science? While many factors have been considered in depth by various educational groups, one of the biggest problems was found to be in the teaching of math to our children. It's not that our teachers are underqualified. Indeed, American teachers have had about twice as many university courses in mathematics as their Japanese counterparts. Not only that, our classes have fewer students per teacher than do classes in Japan, allowing for more individual attention. So what's the problem? The National Research Council report notes the following:

The U.S. curriculum is "repetitious and poorly organized."
Expectation of student performance is too low.
Class time is used ineffectively.
Status of teachers is low.

The problem, as we see it, lies in both the *quality* of teaching and in the *timing* of teaching, which we believe must begin early, at home, as the Japanese have already figured out. It has been reported that more than 80 percent of Japanese children learn to read, write, and count before they even begin elementary school.

The director of the National Institute for Education Research noted: "It is as if [Japanese] mothers had their own built-in curriculum." In fact, a recent issue of *Time* magazine (June 4, 1990) reported on the latest Japanese import: Kumon Mathamatex, a math teaching tool created by Toru Kumon, originally designed to increase his own child's math skills and since developed into a national system of teaching math. While the Kumon system is different from the program we've developed for you and your child, the goal is the same: to teach children the games of math in a way that is fun, builds self-confidence, and will be useful in school and in life. And as the leading math educators emphasize, this process must begin at home.

The school situation is a problem that we can't directly address in this book. What we can do is to convince you that the home is the place to begin your child's education in general and to help you take responsibility for teaching your child math in particular. You can give your child a giant head start, as the Japanese do with their children, by teaching your child the basics at home, not only before he or she begins school, but during it as well. Education is an ongoing process, and the statistics of numerous studies tell us it is unwise to rely on the public school system for your child's education.

But let's not dwell on the negative. There is a positive side to all this, and perhaps the nation's most famous math teacher, Jaime Escalante from Garfield High School in East Los Angeles (featured in the film *Stand and Deliver*), tells us, "We can improve. We can keep kids in school longer and achieve a better result."

3. *Stimulate creative thinking and show the magic in math.*

Most people think of mathematics (and especially arithmetic) as mechanical, laborious, and rigid, with little room for creativity. Sadly, it is sometimes taught that way, but mathematics contains a consistency and inner beauty—a type of magic—that almost defies description.

Take the problem 8 × 12, for instance. One way to solve this is:

$$
\begin{aligned}
8 \times 12 &= 8 \times (10 + 2) \\
&= (8 \times 10) + (8 \times 2) \\
&= 80 + 16 \\
&= 96
\end{aligned}
$$

But there are other ways. For instance, since:

$$12 = 6 \times 2,$$
$$8 \times 12 = 8 \times 6 \times 2$$
$$= 48 \times 2$$
$$= (40 + 8) \times 2$$
$$= 80 + 16$$
$$= 96$$

Or, since:

$$12 = 4 \times 3,$$
$$8 \times 12 = 8 \times 4 \times 3$$
$$= 32 \times 3$$
$$= (30 \times 3) + (2 \times 3)$$
$$= 90 + 6$$
$$= 96$$

What is so intriguing about mathematics is that you can often solve the same problem in many different ways.

Math is like magic. It's awe-inspiring to watch the numbers drop into place, and sometimes you can't believe your eyes. In a sense this is the underlying and deeper goal of this book: to demonstrate that there is magic in numbers and that doing mathematics can be a lot of fun. We want to capture those ideas which encourage children to be creative, for this will benefit them in all aspects of their lives.

There is a certain poetry to math, too. Math is not just a science, it is also an art. There is beauty and shape in math, as there is in a sculpture. There is harmony and symmetry in math, as there is in music. And there is rhyme and meter in math, as there is in poetry. As the mathematician Karl Weierstrass once said, "A mathematician who is not also something of a poet will never be a complete mathematician." In this book we hope to teach you and your child to be both poetic mathematicians and mathematical poets.

PART

I

Getting Excited About Math

"Cheshire-Puss," she began, rather timidly . . . Would you tell me, please, which way I ought to go from here?"

"That depends a good deal on where you want to get to," said the Cat.

"I don't much care where—" said Alice.

"Then it doesn't matter which way you go," said the Cat.

Lewis Carroll, *Alice's Adventures in Wonderland*

CHAPTER

1

Every Child as Mathematician

Alice in Mathland

We have made and will make several references in this book to Lewis Carroll's *Alice's Adventures in Wonderland* and *Through the Looking-Glass* because, as few people realize, Lewis Carroll is the pseudonym of Charles Lutwidge Dodgson, the Oxford University don and mathematician (1832–1898) who befriended Alice Liddell, the young daughter of Dr. Henry George Liddell, dean of one of the many colleges at Oxford. Since our book is about math and children, it is interesting to reflect upon the fact that the many adventures of Alice actually began on July 4, 1862, when Dodgson rowed Alice and her two sisters up the Thames River, "on which occasion I told them the fairy-tale of *Alice's Adventures Underground*, which I undertook to write out for Alice." Decades later an adult Alice recalled that they "used to sit on the big sofa on each side of him while he told us stories, illustrating them by pencil or ink drawings as he went along. . . . He seemed to have an endless store of these fantastical tales, which he made up as he told them, drawing busily on a large sheet of paper all the time."

In fact, Dodgson tells us that he began the whole story with the famed descent by Alice down the rabbit-hole with no plan in mind whatsoever: ". . . in a desperate attempt to strike out some new line of fairy-lore, I had sent my heroine straight down a rabbit-hole, to begin with, without the least idea what was to happen afterwards."

The rest is history, as they say, and Dodgson's books became the most popular children's books of all time. There is an anecdote that Queen Victoria was so taken with the stories that she wrote Dodgson requesting a copy of any of his other works. She was apparently surprised and a bit dismayed to receive a copy of Dodgson's *Syllabus of Plane Algebraical Geometry*.

We wish we had been there to change Queen Victoria's mind about math. We think it is possible to make math fun so that children—and adults—will enjoy it. Mathematics is a game played to better understand the world, and children are natural-born mathematicians and problem solvers. Children like to understand how and why things work. That's why they ask so many questions. Solving math problems is like figuring out a mystery or a puzzle, and children love puzzles. Many children outgrow this fascination with the mysterious by the time they graduate from high school. (Those who don't may just grow up to be scientists and mathematicians!) But this doesn't have to be. With *Teach Your Child Math* you can help nurture and sustain this natural fascination and curiosity about the world in your child and, in the process, rekindle that flame in yourself. We can all learn so much from children that it is a refreshing experience to interact with them on this level.

Playing with Numbers

As an example of learning from children, just recently I was talking to a first-grader who taught *me* a few things about math! Without showing him any math tricks at all, I asked him what $6 + 7$ was. He hadn't completely memorized his addition tables yet, so he didn't automatically know that $6 + 7 = 13$. But he did know that 6 is $5 + 1$ and that 7 is $5 + 2$. He could add $5 + 5$ to get 10. And he could add $1 + 2$ to get 3. Then he just added $10 + 3$ to get 13!

What I learned was just how resourceful children can be in problem solving. Their minds have not yet been indoctrinated with the concept that there is only one way to solve a problem. In reality, there are usually many ways.

There are certainly lots of ways to solve math problems. That's the beauty of math. And children find this very natural—they ask lots of questions, and they are not shy about trying different strategies and coming up with various answers. Psychologists, in fact, have shown that children are much better than adults at using a variety of problem-solving strategies because they are not generally fearful of "making fools of themselves" as most adults are, and consequently they are willing to try any or all solutions to a problem.

One of the problems with the school system is that children are taught that there is a *right* answer and there is a *wrong* answer, and while they are rewarded for coming up with the right answer, they are also sometimes punished for coming up with the wrong answer. The fact is, many problems don't have just one right answer. (We don't mean to imply that all answers are equal but that there may be more than one answer or, more likely, there may be more than one way to *find* an answer.)

For example, with a simple coin demonstration (in chapter 7), you can show your little mathematician why 3×4 is the same as 4×3. Or why 2×6 is the same as 6×2. If your child asks "Why are they the same?" you won't have to say, "Because that's just the way it is." You can just reach into your pocket, pull out 12 coins, and *demonstrate* why it must be true. If you turn math into a game, it becomes not only fun, but understandable.

On this level then, math is a science because we use it to help us understand the causes of things. Human beings, children and adults alike, want to know what is going on around them and why. None other than the great Italian astronomer and mathematician Galileo called mathematics the "language of nature." In this way math is a kind of language that we learn to help us communicate with each other about nature and the cosmos. And, like foreign languages, the language of mathematics can be easily understood by children. In fact, if learning mathematics is like learning a foreign language, then it *is* easier for children to learn—and the earlier you start them on it the better.

Why Teach Your Child Math?

If you have picked up this book and read this far, we assume that you feel it is a good idea to teach your child math. Naturally we couldn't agree more, but why? Exactly why does your child need to know math? Without trying to sound as if we're claiming math will work miracles in your child's life, we can confirm that there are certain benefits likely to result from having played the games of math. For example, your child may be more successful academically, which translates into better grades in school. Your child may be more successful intellectually, which translates into a better job and higher salary. Your child may become a more effective problem solver, which translates into more success in school, on the job, or in any other social situation. Educators call this form of problem solving "critical thinking," and it applies to all sorts of problems, both practical and emotional. Finally, your child may learn to think logically and rationally, which translates into a healthy balance between open-mindedness and skepticism throughout a life filled with ideas and challenges. You don't want your child to be so open-minded that gullibility is the norm; on the other hand, you don't want your child to be so skeptical that no new learning takes place. There is a balance—a happy medium—somewhere between these two extremes, and a basic grounding in problem solving, as this book offers, will help your child know the difference.

How to Use This Book

We have written this book for parents whose children range in age from preschool to the 4th or 5th grade. Obviously this is a fairly broad range of ages, and, even within the same age group, math skills will vary. Thus we've structured the book to flow from easiest to hardest, from the most basic math skills to those more advanced. By doing this we also hope to defuse the math anxiety we all seem to experience at one time or another. By developing a sequence of games from easy to harder, we hope to show you that one game, or math skill, follows from the other. There need be no math anxiety, because if you begin from the beginning, mastery of each stage will build the confidence to move on to the next.

Since this book is for both parents and their children, it is also important to note how it is written. We are writing *to* you, the parent, with the idea that you will then teach what we have taught you about certain math games. On the other hand, we have written the book *for* your child, in a way that assumes neither you nor your child knows anything about math. We are taking the risk of oversimplifying for you, the parent, in order to ensure that all the math concepts covered in this book can be understood by all readers, no matter what their age or their background in math. Thus, the way to use this book is to read a section on your own first, then go through the games and their rules with your child, using either our basic wording to describe math games, or your own—whatever works best for your child.

In the remainder of Part I (chapter 2), we define mathematics as a game and discuss the rules of the game and the best way for you to play the game with your child; we also review the Who, What, Where,

When, and Why of math. In Part Two: Let the Games Begin (chapters 3–8), we introduce you to numerous games of math that you can actually play with your child. We start with the most basic math functions—so basic, in fact, that you probably never considered them as a part of math. But such things as *naming, sorting, comparing, ordering, measuring,* and *counting* (chapters 3 and 4) are a child's first experience with basic math skills, skills that will later develop into more advanced techniques such as *addition, subtraction, multiplication,* and *division,* to be found in chapters 5–8.

But when we say "more advanced," we don't necessarily mean beyond even a preschooler's understanding. Most of the book can be used with a preschooler. In each chapter, and in each step of the way, we assume that your child knows nothing about that particular math game, so we begin at the beginning and work our way up to more difficult problems. But with each step, and your child's understanding of it, comes readiness for the next step, and the next, and so on.

We always begin with practical examples, including lots of visuals, like the pigs, pens, and "pundreds," and then progress to just numbers and symbols. We hope that this sequencing of games will ease your child into being comfortable with numbers so that in school, when she is faced with just the mathematical numbers and symbols, she will recall all the fun she had with the visual examples we used, and try to make schoolwork a game as well.

If you begin to teach your child math before school begins, we believe it will provide your child with a head start, even if she does not completely grasp the concepts in this book. If nothing else, by playing the math games, your child will become familiar with numbers, symbols, and such basic skills as naming, sorting, comparing, ordering, measuring, and counting. And if she learns basic addition and subtraction and some math rules, then school, in many ways, will just reinforce what your child already knows. If she has forgotten some of these rules, school will be a relearning experience, since she will have seen these games before. It only gets better from there. If she does remember many of the math rules, then this book will have been a good primer.

If, on the other hand, you introduce your child to the games in this book after she has started school, this will be a good supplement to school math books. Knowing what these books are like, we believe our presentation of the math rules and games will provide a refreshingly different approach to the problems your child will have already gotten in school.

We want to note here that individual variation between children in math skills is the norm, not the exception. We can't pretend that in one book, and in each chapter, we will meet the exact needs of all children. You need to gauge for yourself how your child is progressing through the various games in each chapter. If your child is too advanced for the most basic games, then skip those and move on to the more advanced games. You will know when to push your child forward, or take a step back, by observing how she is doing with the games. You as a parent will become, in a way, and with our help, your child's math teacher.

We've included numerous appendices so that this book can also serve as a handy guide and reference source for now or in the future. You will find appendices listing *math and science books* and *periodicals* for children and adults, an appendix showing the many *careers* your child can go into with a degree in math (there are more than you will believe!), and, to show you how you can expand your child's interest in math and science, we have included an appendix listing *math, science, and technology museums* by region and state throughout the United States, and another listing *scientific companies* that publish math and science catalogues and distribute teaching tools.

Our main objective in this book is to convey the joy, fun, and feel of numbers. Just telling a kid to look at a set of numbers long enough to memorize them, like a multiplication table, for instance, isn't going to produce a lot of excitement or understanding. We want your child to *understand* the rules of the game of math, so that she can not only play it successfully, she can also have fun playing the game. The rules make sense, so there is no reason to require a child to memorize them. When she can understand them and reason them out, memorization takes place naturally.

Having fun solving problems is the key to teaching children math. In the process, your child can grow up to become a *numerate* adult, as opposed to *innumerate*. Innumeracy is recognized today as a real difficulty for many adults. This isn't, of course, something you need to discuss with your child. Children don't need to know the engineering applications of mathematics, or why this education will make them better adults. As long as math is presented to them in a way that is fun, in a way that they understand, and in a way that they can feel good about, they will quickly find themselves enjoying math, just as they enjoy any game once they've mastered the rules.

CHAPTER

2

Mathematics as a Game

Many people are intimidated by math because they think it involves a lot of memorization of number tables and arcane formulas they will never use in the real world. Such tables are useful, of course, but they should be used only for reference and as guides, not for an *understanding* of math. "Math anxiety" is an actual label that psychologists use to describe a fear of doing math, which results, in part, from being intimidated by such mathematical paraphernalia. Many colleges even offer courses in overcoming math anxiety, and it's no wonder that people need them when they come across such descriptions of math as this one from Merriam-Webster's dictionary: "The science of numbers and their operations, interrelations, combinations, generalizations, and abstractions and of space configurations and their structure, measurement, transformations, and generalizations." But math need not be intimidating. In fact, we can define math very simply in the following way:

Mathematics is a game or series of games played in an attempt to understand the world.

In a way, the various games of math that we will discuss in this book—addition, subtraction, multiplication, and division—are systems for solving problems which help us better understand the world around us. When Galileo said, "The book of nature is written in the language of mathematics," he meant that we need to understand math in order to have a dialogue with nature. When the Nobel prize-winning physicist Richard Feynman said, "If you want to understand nature, you must be conversant with the language in which nature speaks to us," he was talking about mathematics. And just as you wouldn't travel to a foreign country where the people speak a different language and expect to understand their culture without learning the language, you can't expect to understand science and nature without learning their language—the language of mathematics.

The prediction of an eclipse, the sending of a man to the moon, the forecast of the weather, the proper mixing of chemical elements in medicine, the realization of the potential extinction of an animal species, the estimation of the births and deaths in a population in order to set insurance premiums, the approximation of the number of cars traveling on a stretch of highway in order to expedite traffic flow, and so forth, all depend on math. So as you can see, math is not *only* for understanding but for prediction and control as well. The calculus, for example, enables us not only to understand the motion of planets and moons but also to predict their location at any time in the future so well that we can send a spacecraft there and have it land within inches of the projected target. Probabilities and statistics make it possible for us to estimate the actions of extremely complex systems such as the changing weather, population increases and decreases, economic recessions and depressions, business cycle booms and busts, and even how many Americans will get the flu or purchase cars this year. Mathematics is not *just* a game, it is one of the most important games any of us will ever play.

The Rules of the Game

Now that we've defined mathematics as a game or series of games, we need to make you aware of its rules. Since we are not playing one game but many, the rules that follow are really only suggestions on how to make the overall game of math fun for you and your child. Each particular math game, like addition or subtraction, will have certain rules all its own, and we will cover those in subsequent chapters. But in general, here are 10 rules, or guidelines, for playing the overall game of math:

1. **Be upbeat and positive.** Start the math games on a positive note. You and your child are going to have fun, and you've got to convey that to your child through your words and actions.

2. **Approach math as you would any other game.** Set up the math games on the premise that this is like playing computer games, or sports, or any game your child enjoys. You know that if children are enjoying a game, they can play for hours on end without even being aware of the time.

3. **It's okay to say "I don't know."** It isn't necessary for your child to think you are an authority in order to teach him math. In fact, if you approach the subject as if both of you were starting from scratch and you're both going to play this game and learn something from it, it will seem more like a joint effort than a teacher–student relationship. This will keep math more *game-like* and less *school-like.*

4. **Use real-world examples in math problems.** A math word problem can be both intimidating and boring. For example, "If 8 units of something makes up ¼ of the whole, how many units are in the whole?" is a question that has no appeal for a child. But if your child is a basketball fan, you might word the problem like this: "If Magic Johnson scores 8 points in each quarter of a basketball game, how many points will he score for the total game?" This is not only more "user-friendly" and less intimidating, it shows your child how math is a real-world tool used by everyone. In the chapters that follow we will offer such real-world examples whenever appropriate for you to use.

5. **When doing arithmetic, use objects around the house.** When baking or cooking, let your child get involved by measuring ingredients in wholes or in parts, or by counting objects (such as the number of chocolate chips for cookies or the number of pepperoni slices for pizza). The more senses he can use, the easier it will be for him to learn. If your child can not only hear you explain a mathematical concept but also see it, touch it, or even taste it (eating a certain *number* of chocolate chips!), it will leave a far more lasting impression than if he were just counting them by number.

6. **Find similarities in objects.** What do 7 days in the week have in common with 7 months in the year? Yes, they are both numbers

representing the passage of time, but, more important, they share the similarity of the number 7. You can do this sort of comparison quite easily, and it will help your child develop basic math skills. In chapters 3 and 4 we will be dealing with such basic math skills as naming, sorting, comparing, ordering, measuring, and counting. Objects around the house can readily be used for such games. For example, after teaching your child that "pots" are things used for cooking, you can have him compare the pots in terms of their various sizes, or have him order them from large to small, or match them to their covers, and so on. As we shall see in chapter 4, measuring games work wonderfully when doing actual cooking. Whether your child is filling a cup with raisins or counting potatoes, he is doing mathematics physically, so to speak, which is very conducive to learning.

7. **Find the differences in objects.** This exercise is similar to exercise number 6 above, but in this case you might ask such questions as: "How is a basketball different from a baseball? How is a basketball different from a dinner plate? How are the days of the week different from the months in a year? Here you are teaching your child to be discerning and discriminating, rather than just generalizing about things. In mathematics, it is as important to see differences as it is to see similarities. With these two rules, you are essentially "fine-tuning" your child's perceptual skills. It doesn't sound like math directly, but it is a skill that will come in handy in learning. That is why we begin the games of math in chapters 3 and 4 with these sorts of games. Playing with numbers is really a game of playing with similarities and differences. The more your child has acquired this perceptual skill, the easier these math necessities will be learned.

8. **Don't work at any math problem for too long.** Math can be stimulating and a lot of fun when done for the proper length of time. But if done too long, it can be mentally fatiguing for anyone, especially children, whose attention span is considerably shorter than that of adults. Keep the math games short and to the point. Set aside just 15 minutes to play a few math games with your child. And tell children how long you will be playing, so they won't worry that this is going to last all afternoon while their friends are out "having a good time." Not only should you make the game fun but, as they say in show business, "Always leave them asking for more."

9. **Offer a moderate amount of assistance in solving a problem.** If your child gets stuck on a problem and can't solve it immediately, there is a happy medium between doing the problem for your child and ignoring him completely. Offer hints and tips on solving the problem in a way that will lead him to see it for himself. If the child does not make the mental connection himself, learning will not take place. This is an important skill for a parent, which can only come with practice and experience, as every child and every parent–child relationship is different. In time you will learn where that critical point lies between your child's learning *from* you and leaning *on* you.

10. **Have fun!** These rules, or guidelines, are to help you get started in playing the games of math with your child. They are by no means comprehensive, and you may find that some work better than others in your particular circumstances. But, as we keep insisting, math is more than just a game, and in calling it that we don't want to give the impression that it is a frivolous subject. There are a number of things about math that we feel go beyond the "game" aspect and point to the deeper and richer side of the subject— what we shall call the who, what, where, when, and why of math.

The Who, What, Where, When, and Why of Math

WHO IS MATH FOR? Mathematics is for everyone. As mathematician M. A. Guillen said, "A person without an understanding of mathematics is deprived of any intimate comprehension of our complex technological world. He is merely a spectator rather than a participant in the world." But mathematics is not only for the engineer, the technical person—it is for the artist, too, and for the person who enjoys discovering things, looking for patterns, looking for consistency and structure. Often, unfortunately, it is not taught that way. Schools are hung up on the mechanics or the process of doing math, while very little emphasis is put on understanding or appreciating its concepts. Yet, once the concepts are understood, not only will mathematics become more meaningful, but the practical applications will come easily.

For example, in calculus you may be asked to find the area under a curve. Just doing the math is hard enough, but you become even more frustrated when you have no clue as to why anyone would even *want* to find the area under a curve. But if the area under a curve happens to be the side of a building with a curved roof, and the area under that roof is a series of windows, and finding the area means knowing exactly what size to cut the glass, then you can see why it is important, and the learning becomes a lot more fun. Or suppose you're asked to plot the motion of a point through space. Pretty boring—until you know it's for a multimillion-dollar spacecraft carrying human beings to another planet, with thousands of engineers and other workers depending on your calculations to get the spacecraft to its appointed planet. Suddenly you become much more interested, excited, and careful in doing your math. Imagine how careful NASA mathematicians must be when they do their math!

WHAT IS MATH GOOD FOR?   Mathematics is useful for solving problems. The steps one follows in solving a division problem, for example, are similar in procedure to those one might follow in solving a business problem. Remember those math word problems we all dreaded in high school algebra? If a truck driving down a highway covers 140 miles in 3.5 hours, how long will it take to complete a journey from point A to point B, which are 1,000 miles apart? I can hear you groaning already. But if you run a business that transports fresh fruit from Los Angeles to Albuquerque, New Mexico, and getting paid will depend on getting it there on time, then I have no doubt you will figure this problem out somehow, even if you've never had any math training at all. You will find a way because your livelihood depends on it. And problems like this fill our daily lives. I don't just mean problems like what is 19 times 14, but questions like:

"Should I rent my videotapes at the regular price or pay an annual fee that will allow me to rent them at a lower price?"

"Which auto insurance policy provides the best coverage?"

"Is the car salesman overcharging me on my monthly auto payments?"

Our lives are affected by other people's solutions to math problems, ranging from how much we pay for a loaf of bread to how long we have to wait at a red light to how much tax is taken out of our paychecks to—you name it.

WHERE CAN YOU GO WITH MATH?   Almost anywhere. That is why Wall Street businesses and law and medical schools actively recruit students with strong math backgrounds into their programs. Why? Because if you can solve mathematical problems you are better equipped to solve the nonmathematical problems that abound in life. Everyone's job involves solving some kind of problem, and mathematics exercises those problem-solving muscles in your brain.

We've all grappled with math problems sometime in our lives, and when we meet someone with formal training, or someone who has mastered mathematical concepts, we're impressed. So are potential employers and personnel departments. In appendix 4 we've included a huge list of careers for people with a degree in math. To name just a few, they include accounting, astronomy, business, economics, electrical engineering, law, medicine, physics, psychology, public health sciences, public policy and management, architecture, aerospace research, banking, biology, chemistry, computer science, data control, cost estimating, geology, geography, cartography, industrial traffic managing, instrument making, market research, meteorology, pension fund analysis, optometry, surveying, technical writing, and on, and on, and on. The list is seemingly endless because math applies to so many things.

WHEN DO YOU NEED MATH?   Most of the time. But is everyone out there always solving problems mathematically? No. Most adults are not out there doing mathematics, but they *are* solving problems. Even simple tasks, such as tipping at a restaurant, may be cumbersome if you don't have at least a basic understanding of math. It can be a nerve-racking process while your guests sit there watching you stare at the check wondering how much to tip. Now if it is a straight 10% this is simple enough because you just move the decimal point over one place. So if the check is $17.52, the tip comes to $1.75. Some places, however, expect a 20% tip, but that's almost as easy because you can just quickly double the 10% figure and get $3.50. But most restaurants today expect you to tip 15%, which is a little harder. If you've got a calculator the problem is easy: 15% of $17.52 is $2.62. But, of course, you won't always have your calculator handy, nor is it necessarily always appropriate to use it in certain settings, which gets back to this section's question and answer: When do you need math? And the answer is, most of the time. So if multiplying .15 times $17.52 doesn't bring a quick response from you, there's another way. Since 10%, or $1.75, is so easy to get, and 5% is just half of that, or about 90¢, you can add 10% + 5%, or $1.75 + 90¢, to get a tip of $2.65, which is almost exactly 15%.

WHY MATHEMATICS? For all of the above reasons, and more. Yes, math is fun. Yes, math is useful. Yes, math will make you and your child better and more critical thinkers. But there is more. Math is beautiful. Mathematics really does describe, in so many ways, the workings of the universe, and all the actions within it, including those of people. And when you have something that comprehensive, that all-encompassing, it's hard not to be impressed with it all. As the British astronomer and mathematician Sir James Jeans said, "The Great Architect of the Universe now begins to appear as a pure mathematician."

PART

II

Let the Games Begin

"I mean, what *is* an un-birthday present?"

"A present given when it isn't your birthday, of course."

Alice considered a little. "I like birthday presents best," she said at last.

"You don't know what you're talking about!" cried Humpty Dumpty. "How many days are there in a year?"

"Three hundred and sixty-five," said Alice.

"And how many birthdays have you?"

"One."

"And if you take one from three hundred and sixty-five, what remains?"

"Three hundred and sixty-four, of course."

Humpty Dumpty looked doubtful. "I'd rather see that done on paper," he said.

Alice couldn't help smiling as she took out her memorandum-book, and worked the sum for him:

$$\begin{array}{r} 365 \\ \underline{1} \\ 364 \end{array}$$

Humpty Dumpty took the book, and looked at it carefully. "That seems to be done right—" he began.

"You're holding it upside down!" Alice interrupted.

"To be sure I was!" Humpty Dumpty said gaily, as she turned it round for him. "I thought it looked a little queer."

—Lewis Carroll, *Through the Looking-Glass*

CHAPTER

3

Begin at the Beginning: Games of Naming, Sorting, and Comparing

Before we "let the games begin," we must recognize that math games actually start with some very basic functions. For example, before you teach your child to add, subtract, multiply, and divide, he must have certain basic skills in order to handle the juggling of numbers around in his head. Naming, sorting, and comparing are the most basic, and we begin this section at the beginning, with a chapter on these skills, and then move to slightly more advanced skills in the next chapter on ordering, measuring, and counting. *Then* we will be ready to move onward to addition, subtraction, multiplication, and division.

Naming

Naming is one of the first and most fundamental cognitive functions your child will learn, and it begins long before school. In fact, the very development of language depends a great deal on the naming of objects, experiences, and people. Until she can use the common labels we all attach to the variety of things in our environment, it will be difficult for your child to show much development of mathematical understanding. By the time your child is a year and a half to two years old, she will have developed a fairly elaborate vocabulary of names and nouns for most of the important people, objects, and experiences in her immediate environment: Mommy, Daddy, Grandma, Grandpa, dog, cat, arm, leg, drink, food, eat, bottle, and so on. It will take a little longer for her to realize that some of these words are the names of animals, while others are the parts of the body, while still others belong to inert objects.

Sorting

Once your child has learned the names of objects and can easily recall them upon demand, she is ready to begin sorting and, in fact, probably already does so. Sorting involves *grouping* the named objects into their appropriate categories, based on any number of characteristics. Animals are grouped differently from rocks, but dogs are also in a different category from cats. Sorting comes naturally, once a large number of named objects becomes a part of your child's regular vocabulary.

Comparing

As you can already see, comparing is really part of naming and sorting, since the very process of assigning two objects different names means they must somehow be different, which requires the skills of sorting them apart and making comparisons between them. Thus your child can see that animals and rocks not only have different names but they belong in different groups and, in comparison, there are many characteristics that they do not share.

Naming, Sorting, and Comparing Games

The first step in your child's mathematical development, then, is to learn to name, sort, and compare objects. Since all three skills interact, we will play games that use all three. For example, you need to get your child thinking about the properties or characteristics that make a cat a cat and *not* a dog or a ball. To do so, you might try this word game, which is good for practicing all three tasks—naming, sorting, and comparing. In using these skills we are naming an object, then sorting it with others like it and apart from other things that are not like it, and then making comparisons between them. The dialogue is based on how your child might respond to your questions, so feel free to adapt your approach.

Why Is a Dog a Dog?

(You can use a cat or any other object you want if you don't have a dog.)

PARENT [holding a dog]:   What's this?

CHILD *[aged three]:*   A dog.

PARENT: How do you know it's a dog?

CHILD: Because it's furry and has ears?

PARENT: Yes, that's right. It is furry and has ears. What else has it got?

CHILD: It's got four legs and a tail.

PARENT: Okay, what color is it?

CHILD: It's black.

PARENT: Is the dog alive?

CHILD: Yes.

PARENT: How do you know it's alive?

CHILD: Because it's warm and moves around.

PARENT [holding up a ball]:   How is the dog different from this ball?

CHILD: The ball is round and the dog is long.

PARENT: What else is different about the ball?

CHILD: The ball is hard.

PARENT: Is the dog hard?

CHILD: No, the dog is soft.

PARENT [holding up a fork]:   What's this?

CHILD: That's a fork.

PARENT: How do you know it's a fork?

CHILD: Because . . . uh, it is.

PARENT: Why is it?

CHILD: You told me so.

PARENT: How is the fork different from the ball and the dog?

CHILD: I don't know.

PARENT: Well, what does the fork look like compared with the ball and dog?

CHILD: Uh, the fork is small and long and has points at the end.

PARENT: That's right. And as you can see, the ball is made out of rubber, the fork is made out of metal, and the dog is made up of flesh and bones. So they are all different because they are different shapes, different sizes, and made out of different things.

What Is It?

The next game is to play the previous game backward. That is, hide several objects that your child is already familiar with in a bag. Then reach in and grab an object, describe it in words, and see if your child can guess what it is without seeing it. The more characteristics you use the better your child will get at naming, sorting, and comparing these various objects. In mathematics we use all three skills when we name numbers (a "1," "2," "3"), when we sort them into different groups (all single-digit numbers, or all "2s," or whatever), and when we compare them (essentially seeing their differences and using these differences to reach mathematical conclusions). Then we can begin ordering, measuring, and counting them. Let's try another game, this one focused on sorting.

Spoons

PARENT [holding up a spoon]:   What's this?

CHILD: A spoon.

PARENT: What makes it a spoon?

CHILD: It's round on the end.

PARENT [pointing to a pile of silverware]:   Can you find another spoon in this pile of silverware?

CHILD [pointing to another spoon]:   Here's one.

PARENT: That's right. Now, can you find a knife?

CHILD [picking up a knife]:   Here's a knife.

PARENT: How is the knife different from the spoon?

CHILD: It's long and sharp and you can cut yourself with it.

PARENT: Can you find another knife?

Child picks up another knife. Continue game with other objects.

Feelies

Naming, sorting, and comparing is not *just* a visual process. Child psychologists, in fact, tell us that before children learn the shapes of objects by looking at them, they grab them, feel them, put them in their mouths—in other words, they *feel* the shapes of objects. (A study with blind-since-birth adults who were given a chance to see again through surgery showed that they were initially unable to discriminate between a ball, a cube, and a pyramid by sight alone. They first had to *feel* the shapes because that is how they had learned about shapes as children.) In this game have your child feel a shape that she cannot see by placing an object in a bag and having her reach in and try to guess what it is. After she *names* the object, have her describe its characteristics in as much detail as possible. After getting the correct name, she can then *sort* and *compare* the object with others if you place a bunch of objects in front of her and have her take the object out of the bag and place it with a matching object. But have her point to the correct object in front of her that matches the one in the bag *before* she pulls it out of the bag. This will help sharpen her discriminatory powers of sorting and comparing.

Advanced Feelies

In this slightly more advanced game, put several objects in a bag, all of which are the same except one. The task of the game is for your child to name the object that is the odd one out. Thus you have him name the odd object, describe it, and then explain how it is different from the other objects, which he should also describe. This game nicely exercises all three skills of naming, sorting, and comparing. For example, you might put in a bag four spoons and one fork, or four round shapes and one triangle, or four things to eat and one nonedible object, or four articles of clothing and one rock, or four crayons and one rock, and so forth. The simplest comparisons are obviously by shape or size. More sophisticated comparisons might be made with the *functions* of objects, such as putting four different sizes of plastic measuring cups and one fork in the bag. Since the four measuring cups are themselves different, your child will have to reason to the conclusion that they do share something in common that isn't shape or size, but function (they are used to measure liquids). Use your imagination with this game in practicing any number of such comparisons.

Shapies

"Shapies" is like "Feelies," except instead of naming the object in the bag, have your child describe its shape. Is it round, does it have angles, is it flat, is it long, is it short? For example, put a book in the bag, and even though your child will probably know immediately that it's a book, perhaps she will describe it this way:

CHILD: It's kinda flat, long on one end, short on the other.

PARENT: Does it have angles or curves?

CHILD: Angles.

PARENT: Is the object solid or does it have parts?

CHILD: What do you mean?

PARENT: I mean, is it one solid piece or does it have loose pieces in it?

CHILD: It sorta comes apart and there are pages that flip loose.

PARENT: What object is this shape?

CHILD: A book.

Or try putting a light bulb in a bag. Maybe the questions and answers would go something like this:

PARENT: What shape is this object?

CHILD: It's a light bulb.

PARENT: That's very good, but I want to know what *shape* it is. Can you describe the shape of the light bulb?

CHILD: It's round.

PARENT: Is it round like a ball?

CHILD: Yes.

PARENT: But is it *perfectly* round like a ball?

CHILD: Well, no.

PARENT: How is it different from a ball?

CHILD: It's kinda big on one end and smaller on the other.

PARENT: Are both ends rounded?

CHILD: Yes.

PARENT: So how are they different?

CHILD: The one end is like a big ball and the other end is small and rounded.

PARENT: Very good. Now, what other shape can you feel on the small end? [Meaning the threads that screw into the light socket.]

CHILD: There are metal lines, or kinda bumps on the end.

PARENT: Do you know what these bumps are called?

CHILD: No.

PARENT: This shape is called a spiral. It's like a circle that goes round and round but keeps moving down. Do you know why there is a spiral on the end?

CHILD: So that it goes in the lamp?

PARENT: That's right! The spiral shape helps the light bulb fit in the lamp, and it's metal because the metal is what makes the electricity from the lamp go into the light bulb. Very good. Let's play another game.

Advanced Shapies

"Advanced Shapies" is a little like "Shapies" in that the goal is to help your child describe shapes and learn to name, sort, and compare various shapes, but this time you will give your child the name of the shape and his task is to find an object that fits that shape. For example, if the shape you choose is a circle, you will ask him to find an object in the house that is shaped like a circle. Perhaps he will point to anything that is round shaped, like a cup or drinking glass, or the end of a telephone, or the base of a lamp, or a coin. This is a fun game for your child because he can run around the house looking for things (a kind of Easter-egg hunt). You might try the following shapes:

Circle, or round.

Square, or cube.

Rectangle.

Triangle.

Ellipse (like an egg).

What soon becomes interesting in this game is how many items in your home can be reduced to just a limited number of shapes, basically those listed above. For a more interesting and fun game, go to the next one, in which we move beyond just shapes.

Where Is It? What Is It?

In this game you and your child will play by the same rules as in the previous game, but this time have your child go through various objects in the house that match a whole variety of characteristics. In addition to the shapes listed in the previous game, have her find things by color, or size, or texture, and so on. For example, have her point to all objects that are red. Or have her touch all objects she thinks are large or small. Try this game with the following list of characteristics:

Shape (circle, square, rectangle, triangle, ellipse).

Size (large, small, narrow, wide, tall, short).

Texture (rough, smooth, hairy, hairless, slippery, sticky).

Color (red, blue, green, brown, beige, purple, black).

Sound (makes noise that is loud, soft, shrill).

Position (on top of, below, inside, outside, above, behind, high, low).

Orientation (right side up, upside down, facing in, facing out).

For example, have your child find something in the shape of a circle that also makes a noise and is inside the house. This could be a clock, because it is round, makes a tick-tock noise, and hangs on the wall. Or something that is rectangular, large, and smooth might be a window.

Helping Mommy and Daddy

This is essentially the same game as "Where Is It? What Is It?" except it is more practical because you will be having your child help you with daily activities and chores around the house which require skills of naming, sorting, and comparing. For example, the next time you go to the store to buy groceries, have your child take them out of the bag, name them all while he puts them on the table, and have him sort them on the table according to their shapes. So round things go together, such as cans and fruit, and square things go together, such as cereal boxes and milk cartons. Then have him help you put them away, which is a game of sorting and comparing because they won't be put away according to size and shape, but according to more complex criteria, such as whether they need to be cold (milk, juice, meat, ice cream), or what sort of food they are (the cereal boxes all go in one cupboard, the fruit all goes in one bowl), or whether they go in the pantry or in the cupboard, and so forth.

You can also play this game with other home projects, such as sorting out the clothes after a wash—the socks are paired and go in one drawer, while the underwear goes in another drawer. Or in the garage, where tools are sorted by their size or function and put into various drawers or on shelves.

Basically, our lives are relatively organized around the naming, sorting, and comparing of objects that are of use to us, and you can teach your child the fundamentals of these skills by just looking around your environment and honing your child's intellectual development through these simple games.

CHAPTER

4

How Many Are There? Games of Ordering, Measuring, and Counting

Now that your child has mastered the beginning skills of mathematical reasoning—naming, sorting, and comparing—it's time to move on to slightly more advanced skills—ordering, measuring, and counting. This is the perfect transition into what most of us consider the start of math—namely, arithmetic, which includes addition, subtraction, multiplication, and division. In this chapter we will be playing games similar to those in chapter 3, though what your child does with the objects in the games will require different mental processes.

Ordering

"Ordering" means describing and classifying our environment into a meaningful pattern we can understand, or get our mind around. Ordering is more than just sorting or comparing, because it requires that the objects be sorted and compared in a particular sequence, or line of order. For example, ordering is the sorting of objects not only by size, but by a ranking of size from small to large. So perhaps after you have your child sort the tools in the garage according to size, you will then have her put them in order from the largest down to the smallest.

Measuring

While the precise measuring of various objects by their exact weight, height, or size will probably have to come later in your child's intellectual development (such as learning the standard units of measure—miles, grams, centimeters, etc.), there are a number of measuring skills that you can teach your child in his primary years that will help him in the years to come. For example, cooking is a great way to get started as it requires the measuring of ingredients. You can't expect your child to measure 4.5 ounces of butter, of course, but you can teach him how to add 1 cup of milk, 2 tablespoons of sugar, 3 teaspoons of water, or whatever, to what you're cooking. These measurements, while not scientific, are indeed mathematical and get your child used to the idea of measuring things in comparison with something else—by a standard we have all agreed to use, such as the measurements in a recipe.

Counting

Counting is the climax of the previously learned skills of naming, sorting, comparing, ordering, and measuring. Actually, counting and measuring go hand in hand, but it is a smoother transition to put counting between measuring and addition (the next chapter). In counting games we will practice the skills your child needs to have grasped in order to be able to count accurately so that he can then manipulate numbers in a more sophisticated way. Counting also incorporates sorting, as once the socks (for example) are sorted apart from the underwear and the shirts, it is natural to count both the number of sorted piles and the number of items in each pile.

Ordering Games

Putting things in the right order is important for children of all ages. Your toddler would surely be amused if you tried to put his undershirt on him after you put on his sweater, or if you put on his socks over his shoes! This is a form of ordering, and, as you can readily see, it's a skill that is not only important for mathematical reasoning but one that children begin to learn very early—as soon as they learn to dress, in fact.

As they grow older, children will use cooking recipes, follow directions, read instructions, and so forth. These are all sequenced activities in which the order of things makes an important difference. A sequence is a particular form of ordering in which a number of events are ordered according to time. And it's a mathematical process. Your child will put on his underwear and socks *first,* then put on his pants and shoes *second.* He will put on his shirt *before* he puts on his jacket. Here are some sequencing games to try with your child.

Which Came First?

In this game have your child sit in a chair or on the sofa. Then ask her to close her eyes and listen to the different sounds you are going to make. Now ask her to tell you which sound came first, second, third, and so on.

Begin with an easy sequence of just two sounds:

1. Clap your hands.
2. Stamp your foot on the ground.

If your child knows what *first, second, third* means, then the game shouldn't be too difficult. If you need to teach her this, then do so before playing the game. You can do this by asking her which noise came *before* or *after* another noise. *Before* can be *first, after* can be *second,* or *last.* Once this is learned, you are ready to play the game. You might try playing it like this:

PARENT: Which sound came first?

CHILD: Uh, the clap.

PARENT: That's right. Very good. Now, which sound came second?

CHILD: The foot sound.

PARENT: Great! You got it right. Which sound was last?

CHILD: What do you mean?

PARENT: I mean, what was the *last* sound you heard?

CHILD: Uh, your foot hitting the ground.

PARENT: Absolutely right! So you see, when there are only two sounds, the second sound is also the last sound. Now let's try another one.

This time make these three sounds:

1. Whistle.
2. Snap your fingers.
3. Bark like a dog.

The game might be played like this:

PARENT: Okay, which sound came first *this* time?

CHILD: You whistled.

PARENT: Good! Which sound came second?

CHILD: You barked like a dog.

PARENT: No, that's not right. I barked third. What sound came second?

CHILD: Do the noises again.

[Make the three sounds in sequence again.]

PARENT: Which sound came first?

CHILD: The whistle.

PARENT: Right. Now, which sound came *second*?

CHILD: You snapped your fingers.

PARENT: Very good. That's right. Which sound came last?

CHILD: The bark.

PARENT: Yes. Good. Now, which sound came *third*?

CHILD: Uh . . . the bark?

PARENT: That's right. Do you know why?

CHILD: No.

PARENT: Because in this case last was third, not second, because there were three sounds, and last is always the last noise you hear no matter how many there are. Does that make sense?

CHILD: Yes, I think so.

PARENT: Well, let's play one more game and see.

This time make four sounds:

1. Hit two spoons together.
2. Slap your leg.
3. Scream (not too loud).
4. Whisper.

The game might go something like this:

PARENT: Which sound came last?

CHILD: The whisper.

PARENT: Which sound came first?

CHILD: The spoons.

PARENT: Very good. Now, which sound came second?

CHILD: Uh . . . you slapped your leg.

PARENT: What about the third sound? Which sound came third?

CHILD: Scream.

PARENT: That's right. Do it. Scream.

CHILD: [She screams and then laughs.]

PARENT: Now, pay attention. Which sound came fourth?

CHILD: Fourth?

PARENT: The one that came after the third noise—the scream.

[Repeat the noises if necessary, or give a hint by whispering the question.]

CHILD: The whisper.

PARENT: But which one was *last*?

CHILD: The whisper.

PARENT: Can you tell me how the whisper can be both the fourth and the last noise?

CHILD: Because you said that the last noise is the one heard last no matter how many noises there are.

What Did You Do When You Woke Up?

This game is also an ordering game, but this time you will have your child describe what he did this morning after he woke up from his sleep. You can help teach him numbers (and counting) by asking him:

PARENT: What was the first thing you did when you woke up this morning?

CHILD: I went to the bathroom.

PARENT: What was the *second* thing you did?

CHILD: I brushed my teeth.

PARENT: Good! Then what? What did you do *third*?

CHILD: Uh, I don't remember.

PARENT: Well, let's think. After you brushed your teeth you came out of the bathroom, and then where did you go?

CHILD: I went back into my room and played with my toys.

PARENT: So what was the *third* thing you did this morning?

CHILD: I played with my toys.

PARENT: How about *fourth* ? What was the *fourth* thing you did this morning?

CHILD: Uh, I ate some cereal.

Now go back through the list again, but this time around you describe what your child did and have him tell you what position in the order it was. For example:

PARENT: You did four things this morning. One of them was going to the bathroom. In the order of the four things you did this morning, which was going to the bathroom?

CHILD: First.

PARENT: Right. How about eating cereal?

CHILD: Uh, fourth?

PARENT: That's correct! Good. Now, what about when you brushed your teeth?

CHILD: That was third, I think.

PARENT: Let's run through that again. What did you do after you went to the bathroom?

CHILD: Oh, I brushed my teeth.

PARENT: Right. So what position in the order was brushing your teeth?

CHILD: Second.

PARENT: Very good. Well done.

You can also ask other types of questions, such as which one came *before, after, followed by, next, then,* and so on. These are all positional, or ordering, labels. The following game with beads is also a good game for these ordering sequences.

The Bead Game

This game is simple to play and very instructive for learning and practicing the skill of ordering. Get a string and a bunch of colored beads, and thread six beads on the string. Let's say they are green, red, yellow, blue, black, and white. With this setup you can play the game we have just been playing by asking such questions as:

Which bead is first?

Which bead is second?

Which bead is third?

Which bead is fourth?

Which bead is fifth?
Which bead is sixth?
Which bead comes after the green bead?
Which bead comes before the white bead?
Which bead is last?
Which bead is second to the last?
What color follows the red bead?
What colored beads are next to the yellow bead?

There are many varieties to these games of ordering. For example, you can have your child order things by size. Perhaps have him order your pots and pans from small to large, having him name them by *first, second,* and so on. Then you can ask such questions as:

Which pan is the smallest?
Which pan is the largest?
Which pan is in the middle?
Which pan is first?
Which pan is last?

You can use any number of kitchen or garage items for any number of ordering games that can be based on those above.

Measuring Games

It is one thing for your child to be able to pick out the biggest and the smallest, the first and the last, from a set of objects. It is quite another to be able to say which one has the least or the most, or to be able to measure the tallest or the shortest in some specified units on a ruler. "Measuring" is the word that refers to this skill where size, shape, weight, and so forth, are related to certain units that our culture has agreed to call such measurements—as in pounds, kilometers, inches, centimeters, and so forth. Specific measuring and the memorization of these various units of measurement will probably come later in your child's development. For now, there are some games to play that will help your child get started on this important mathematical task.

Let's Measure Cookies

In this measuring game you can teach your child this math skill by doing something he will surely enjoy—making cookies. Here's the recipe for Peanut Butter Crinkles:

1/4 cup peanut butter
1/4 cup butter
1/2 cup brown sugar
1/2 cup sugar
1 egg
1 teaspoon vanilla
1 cup sifted flour
1/2 teaspoon salt
1 teaspoon soda

Cream peanut butter with butter until soft. Add sugars gradually, continue to beat until light and fluffy. Add egg and vanilla—beat well. Resift flour with salt and soda; add in 2 parts and beat well after each. Drop batter by teaspoonfuls 2 inches apart on greased baking sheet. Press down on each cookie with a fork, then press a second time so that ridges are at right angles. Bake at 350 degrees for 8–10 minutes. Make 4-1/2 dozen cookies.

Here you have a great game for learning how to measure, which will also be quite rewarding when you are finished. You and your child can eat the results of the measuring game. As you go through each ingredient and measure it, have your child actually do the measuring, pouring, and so forth. He may not be able to do it at first, but if you point out how much and then have him do it, he will eventually learn.

For example, take the 1/4-cup measuring cup and have him scoop out enough peanut butter to fill the cup. Have him tell you how much peanut butter there is in the cup ("there is one-quarter cup of peanut butter") and do this with each ingredient. Show him the measuring spoons and have him pick out the 1/2 teaspoon. Then let him pour the salt into the spoon and level it off just right. Have him turn the dial on the oven up to 350 degrees, and show him how to watch the clock or timer so that 8–10 minutes pass before you and he check how the cookies are doing. All of these activities will help him learn about and get used to dealing with numbers, fractions, and a variety of measuring skills.

What Kind of Measure Is It?

In this game you will ask your child which of the following measuring skills are necessary for baking cookies. Then tell him what these measuring skills are called. For example: "Do we use heat for baking cookies?" The answer, of course, is yes, and the measuring skill is called "temperature." Here are the measuring skills and the questions you are to ask you child:

LENGTH: "Do we need to know how long the cookies will be?"

AREA: "Do we need to know how much space is needed between the cookies when we bake them?

VOLUME: "Do we need to know how much cookie dough to use?"

WEIGHT: "Do we need to know how much the cookies weigh?"

TIME: "Do we need to know how long to cook the cookies?"

TEMPERATURE: "Do we use heat for baking cookies?"

CAPACITY: "Do we need to know how many cookies our baking sheet will hold?"

SPEED: "Do we have to know how fast the cookies bake?"

You could play this game with your child using any number of things. Try describing the family car:

LENGTH: "How long is the car?" (You could measure the length using a long tape measure or by walking it off in steps with your child.)

AREA: "How much of the ground does the car cover?"

VOLUME: "How much of the garage does the car take up?" (You can give your child a rough estimate of volume by saying something like: "The car takes up half the garage.")

WEIGHT: "Is the car heavy?"

TIME: "What do we do with a car that requires keeping time?" (You could answer something like: "We often measure distances in how long it takes us to get somewhere. For example, how far is it to the store? It is 10 minutes, meaning it takes 10 minutes to drive to the store.)

TEMPERATURE: "Does the car ever get hot?" And: "How does the car keep cool when it gets too hot?"

SPEED: "How do we know how fast a car can go?"

Counting Games

Counting is not as simple as it may seem at first. There is a big difference between your child's being able to say out loud: "One, two, three, four, five, six," and actually counting six objects in front of her. So while she may be able to count out loud, she may not yet be able to count objects. In this section we look at the skills your child needs to be able to count accurately. Then we look at more complex aspects of counting, such as representing numbers and counting with large numbers.

"How Many" and "How Much"

In chapter 3 your child learned to sort objects. It is important to be able to sort because we are interested in finding similarities and differences between objects in the world. But what else can we say about these objects? Well, for starters, we can say that there are *more* of some and *fewer* of others. We usually speak of *how many* there are of something when there is a set of distinct items that can be counted, such as cookies, people, spoons, and so forth. But, if we are dealing with quantities that can't be separated into individual pieces, we say *how much* there is of something. It isn't surprising that children often confuse these two, and the first thing we need to do is note that *counting* deals with measuring *how many* items there may be of something.

It is important that we also note here, however, that the ability to count accurately may require the ability to "conserve numbers." This is the ability to recognize that the quantity of something remains the same even when it is moved in position or changed in shape. In other words, 10 spoons are 10 spoons no matter whether they are spread out on a table or piled up in a drawer. A cup of milk is a cup of milk, regardless of whether the milk is in a cup, a glass, or poured out on the ground. The amount of the material is "conserved." For young children, it may seem that there are more spoons when they are spread out on the table than when they are bunched up in a drawer. Or there may seem to be more milk when the cup of milk is poured into a small glass and fills it up than when it is poured into a huge glass and fills only a little of it.

A possible reason for this may be that children's notions of "how many" and "how much" may be different from those of adults. For example, they may say that three large cookies are "more" than four small cookies because the big cookies look larger than the small ones or that you can't add tigers and lions. Many preschools try to teach children these skills, but the fact is, whether they are formally taught or not, all children learn to conserve numbers by about age six. There is much individual variation among children on this, however, so you might as well try the math games anyway, just to see what happens, and perhaps a little practice will help your child learn to conserve numbers more quickly.

Onesies and Twosies

Show your child the various sets of objects on the following pages and have him count how many there are in each set. He should see that even though the objects are different, they share a similarity in *how many* there are of *each*.

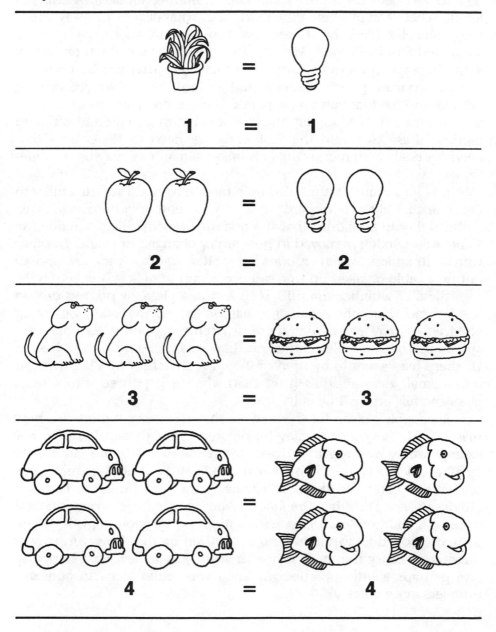

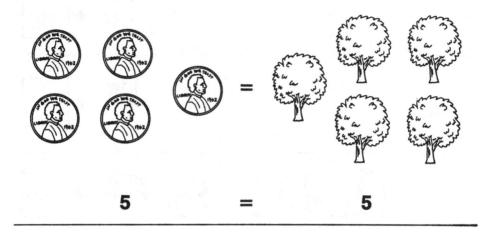

5   =   5

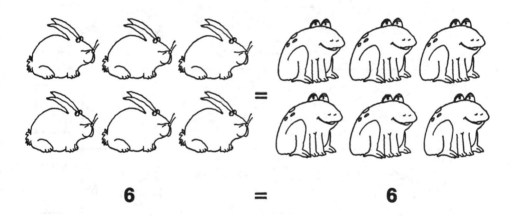

6   =   6

Let's Count to Ten

For this next set of pictures, get out some ruled notebook paper and have your child write down on each line how many there are of each object. Point to the set of objects and ask her, "How many are there?" and then have her write down the number. You may, if you wish, photocopy the pages in this book and then have your child actually write in the boxes. But we recommend you don't have your child write in the book itself because it is our experience that parents and children go back to play these games many times, and once the book is written in it becomes useless for future game playing.

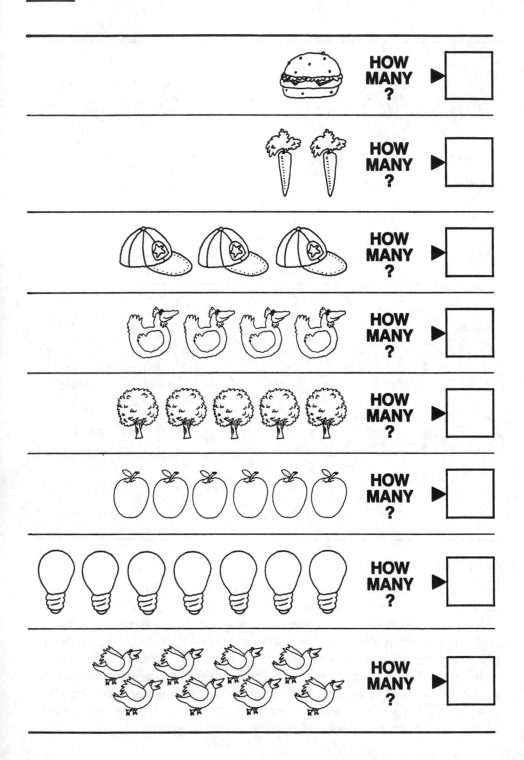

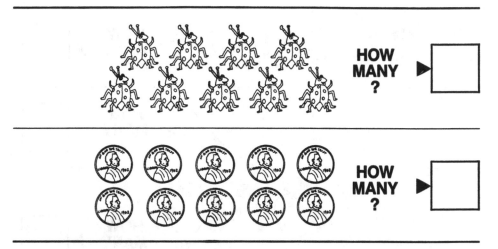

How Many Are There?

In this game the objects grouped together are not in numerical order, from one to ten. They are instead all mixed up so your child will have to assign them a number out of order, thus pushing the skill a little further. Once again, either use ruled notebook paper or photocopy the pages and use those.

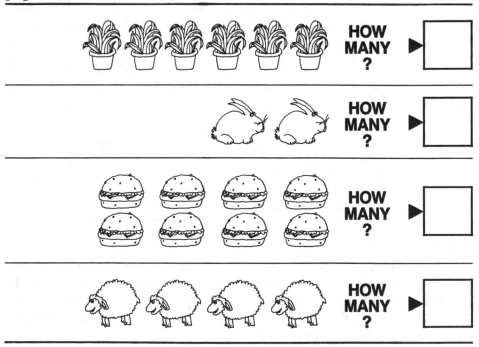

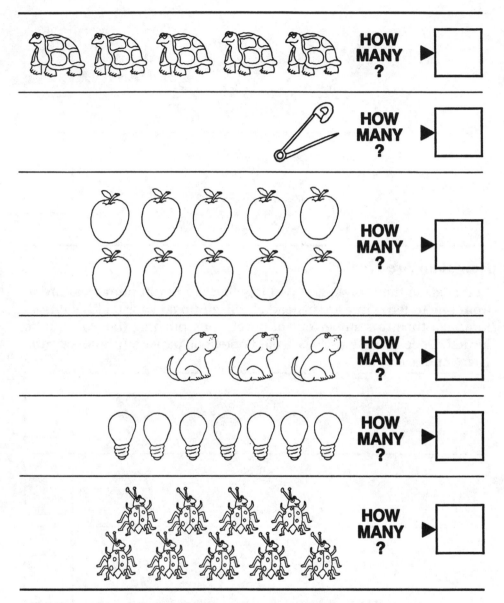

Mixing and Matching

This game is an extension of the game we just played, but now we've not only mixed up the order of the objects and animals to be counted, but we've mixed up the kinds of objects and animals in each set of objects. So now your child will have to "conserve" the number in each *set,* no matter what objects are in them.

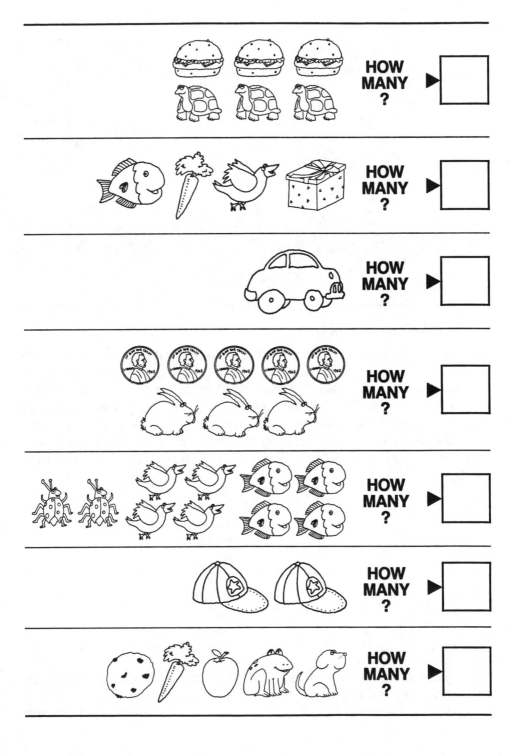

How High Can You Count?

Ask your child how high he can count. He will usually come up with some specific figure. But with the number chart below you can show him that he can count much higher than he thought he could. In fact, it is very easy to show that he can count as high as he wants to because, as you can see in the chart, once your child has mastered counting from 1 to 10, the whole thing just keeps repeating itself and your child only has to learn a few new names. The new names include:

Eleven	Twenty
Twelve	Thirty
Thirteen	Forty
Fourteen	Fifty
Fifteen	Sixty
Sixteen	Seventy
Seventeen	Eighty
Eighteen	Ninety
Nineteen	One hundred

Once your child has mastered this vocabulary he can increase his ability to count a thousandfold! We're not kidding! It's easy.

Teach your child that after ten comes *eleven,* which is just 10 with a 1 in place of the 0. *Twelve* is just 10 with a 2 in place of the 0. *Thirteen* sounds like "three-teen," and it is a 10 with a 3 in place of the 0. Then fourteen—it sounds like "four-teen," and it is a 10 with a 4 in place of the 0. *Fifteen, sixteen, seventeen, eighteen,* and *nineteen* work the same way. Now he just has to memorize *twenty.* Then he can start counting over, except he puts the word *twenty* at the beginning: *twenty-one, twenty-two, twenty-three. . . . And thirty* is easy to remember because it sounds like three; then *thirty-one, thirty-two, thirty-three. . . . And forty, fifty, sixty, seventy, eighty,* and *ninety* follow the same principle. After ninety-nine comes *one hundred.* He can then count all the way to *two hundred* by counting from 1 to 99, but putting the words *one hundred* before each number: *one hundred one, one hundred two, one hundred three . . . one hundred ninety-nine.* Next comes *two hundred,* followed by *two hundred one, two hundred two, two hundred three . . . two hundred ninety-nine,* followed by *three hundred,* and so on up to *nine hundred ninety-nine.*

Once he has mastered this, the next step is easy. The next number is *one thousand,* followed by *one thousand one, one thousand two, one thousand three . . . one thousand nine hundred ninety-nine.* This is followed by *two thousand, two thousand one, two thousand two, two thousand three . . . two thousand nine hundred ninety-nine.* The possibilities are endless. (See the number tables below. A quick glance at these tables will demonstrate how you and your child can count from *one* to any number you want.) The object of this game is to make sure your child knows what comes after any number. This leads us to our next game.

The Counting Game

The Counting Game goes like this: "What comes after—?" So you might begin by asking your child: "What comes after *one?*" Play this game moving up the number scale, but don't ask every number, because that would just be asking your child to count from one to whatever, and this is supposed to be a fun game. So begin by asking what comes after *one,* then *six,* then *fourteen,* and so on as far as you like, but keep it in sequence at first, from small to large numbers. Then mix them up by asking what comes after *seven,* then *two,* then *forty-seven,* then *twenty-three,* then *ninety-nine,* and so on.

Once she has mastered this part of the game, it is time to teach your child the symbols for the numbers, particularly 1, 2, 3, 4, 5, 6, 7, 8, 9, 10. On the next page we have reproduced a number table that gives both the symbol and the number name under the symbol, so that you can show your child the connection between the symbol and the number name.

Start off first by having your child count up with you to a hundred on the number table, you pointing to the number while your child says the number, or you can count together, or your child can even point to the number as she says it.

Next, play the game by pointing to numbers out of sequence on the number table, and have your child tell you the number. You point to 68 and she will tell you "sixty-eight."

Then, you say the number out loud and have your child point out where the number is on the table. For example, you say "forty-seven," and your child points to 47 on the number table.

Finally, you say the number out loud and have your child write down the number on a piece of paper. For example, you say "twenty-six," and your child writes down 26.

Number Table

1 ONE	2 TWO	3 THREE	4 FOUR	5 FIVE	6 SIX	7 SEVEN	8 EIGHT	9 NINE	10 TEN
11 ELEVEN	12 TWELVE	13 THIRTEEN	14 FOURTEEN	15 FIFTEEN	16 SIXTEEN	17 SEVENTEEN	18 EIGHTEEN	19 NINETEEN	20 TWENTY
21 TWENTY-ONE	22 TWENTY-TWO	23 TWENTY-THREE	24 TWENTY-FOUR	25 TWENTY-FIVE	26 TWENTY-SIX	27 TWENTY-SEVEN	28 TWENTY-EIGHT	29 TWENTY-NINE	30 THIRTY
31 THIRTY-ONE	32 THIRTY-TWO	33 THIRTY-THREE	34 THIRTY-FOUR	35 THIRTY-FIVE	36 THIRTY-SIX	37 THIRTY-SEVEN	38 THIRTY-EIGHT	39 THIRTY-NINE	40 FORTY
41 FORTY-ONE	42 FORTY-TWO	43 FORTY-THREE	44 FORTY-FOUR	45 FORTY-FIVE	46 FORTY-SIX	47 FORTY-SEVEN	48 FORTY-EIGHT	49 FORTY-NINE	50 FIFTY
51 FIFTY-ONE	52 FIFTY-TWO	53 FIFTY-THREE	54 FIFTY-FOUR	55 FIFTY-FIVE	56 FIFTY-SIX	57 FIFTY-SEVEN	58 FIFTY-EIGHT	59 FIFTY-NINE	60 SIXTY
61 SIXTY-ONE	62 SIXTY-TWO	63 SIXTY-THREE	64 SIXTY-FOUR	65 SIXTY-FIVE	66 SIXTY-SIX	67 SIXTY-SEVEN	68 SIXTY-EIGHT	69 SIXTY-NINE	70 SEVENTY
71 SEVENTY-ONE	72 SEVENTY-TWO	73 SEVENTY-THREE	74 SEVENTY-FOUR	75 SEVENTY-FIVE	76 SEVENTY-SIX	77 SEVENTY-SEVEN	78 SEVENTY-EIGHT	79 SEVENTY-NINE	80 EIGHTY
81 EIGHTY-ONE	82 EIGHTY-TWO	83 EIGHTY-THREE	84 EIGHTY-FOUR	85 EIGHTY-FIVE	86 EIGHTY-SIX	87 EIGHTY-SEVEN	88 EIGHTY-EIGHT	89 EIGHTY-NINE	90 NINETY
91 NINETY-ONE	92 NINETY-TWO	93 NINETY-THREE	94 NINETY-FOUR	95 NINETY-FIVE	96 NINETY-SIX	97 NINETY-SEVEN	98 NINETY-EIGHT	99 NINETY-NINE	100 ONE HUNDRED

CHAPTER

5

Summing Up:
Addition Games

In the last chapter you and your child baked cookies in order to acquire measuring skills in math. So now you've got a couple of trays of cookies. The reward your child expects for playing this game, of course, is a chance to eat some of the results. But before you freely dole them out, try doing an addition game with the cookies. Take out two plates and set them on the table next to a tray of cookies.

You say: "I'm going to give you four more cookies because you did such a great job, and I'm going to have three cookies."

Then put four cookies on one plate and three on another plate.

Then you say: "Okay, how many cookies are you and I going to eat?"

If your child knows nothing about addition, she will just have to count them all up, which she now knows how to do. You can help her by putting all the cookies on one plate so she can then count up "one, two, three, four, five, six, seven."

What you have just done is introduce your child to the math game of addition. "Addition" is just the process of combining two sets of things together, like cookies, and counting the total number. But after we play addition games for a while, your child will learn her addition numbers so well that she won't have to count. In fact, by the end of this chapter she will be able to add 2-digit and 3-digit numbers without having to count or memorize any addition tables at all!

Getting Ready to Play

Now that your child has mastered the basic games of naming, sorting, counting, comparing, ordering, and measuring, the concept of summing up all these objects may naturally occur to her. Since counting is a basic form of addition, it is the addition games to which we now turn. Since you, too, will be playing these games, prepare yourself with some paper, pencils, and a calculator. You generally won't need a calculator for most of the games in this book, and we do supply answers to all the math games your child will play, but it is handy for checking answers, and since most schools are now using calculators, your child might as well get used to using one to check answers, too.

In this chapter, as well as in those that follow, we present a special visual game of math with pictures of little pigs, so that you can teach your child these basic skills in a "hands-on" way. That is, we don't want you to teach your child the addition, subtraction, multiplication, and division tables right away, because that is too much like school or a textbook, and you are supposed to be having fun with math. To your child, the memorization of math tables looks like the mastering of meaningless facts. What we want to do is show your child how she can discover these facts on her own while playing these games.

So this game we've developed is one that you and your child can play right at the dining room table. Your child will learn math by *doing*. Then, after she has mastered the fun games, the traditional rules will come more naturally to her. Therefore, we suggest that you photocopy the pages on which these games appear.

Playing the Numbers

The word "math" makes most people think of numbers. Well, basically that's true. Numbers are the backbone of math. Numbers by themselves don't do anything, but you can do things to them. That involves *rules* of math, and there are four basic ones: you can add numbers, subtract numbers, multiply numbers, and divide numbers. These four rules are the first things we do with numbers, and this chapter deals with the rule of adding numbers.

In this chapter we want to make the transition from counting to adding by having you show your child that one follows naturally from the other. To help demonstrate this, show your child the pictures of the pigs below, and let's see how counting pigs and adding pigs are similar to each other. Ask your child:

How many pigs are there in this group?

How many pigs are there in this group?

How many pigs are there altogether?

Here is the answer.

Since your child won't know that $4 + 2 = 6$, she will simply count "one, two, three, four, five, six." But she will see that bringing together 4 pigs and 2 pigs makes for a total of 6 pigs, and you can tell her that the way we say this is "$4 + 2 = 6$." Then you can say, "See how addition, or the bringing together of two numbers, is just a different form of counting?"

Let's try some more addition games, this time having your child write down on a separate piece of paper the number of pigs, and also write the plus (+) sign between the numbers. This way you can show your child how to make the shift from the visual image of the pigs to a number that *represents* the pigs, and thus an actual addition problem:

How many pigs are there in this row?

How many pigs are there in this row?

Now let's find out how many pigs there are altogether.

Bringing the rows of pigs together gives us 5 pigs + 3 pigs = 8 pigs.

How many pigs are there in this row?

How many pigs are there in this row?

Now bring the two rows together and what do you get?

You get 7 pigs + 2 pigs = 9 pigs.

Have your child write these problems down mathematically in order to reinforce what she has just learned.

$$5 + 3 = 8$$
and
$$7 + 2 = 9$$

You and your child have now done two different addition problems. Reinforce this by practicing lots of these problems using objects from around the house. For example, you might try the following:

3 spoons + 2 spoons = ? spoons.
5 cups + 4 cups = ? cups.
6 pennies + 5 pennies = ? pennies.
6 forks + 3 forks = ? forks.

Continue playing this game of adding numbers of objects together, keeping the individual numbers being added under 10. If your child does not know her addition tables, she will be counting to get the answers. But that's okay, because if you keep playing the game (practicing the math skill), your child will soon begin to remember these answers and, while having fun, will learn the tables.

Pigs, Pens, and Pundreds

Now we would like to show you a special game to play with your child called "Pigs, Pens, and Pundreds." It will teach him how to play more complicated addition games without having to memorize anything or perform tedious counting.

There is one additional counting skill your child will need for playing this game, and that is adding by tens and hundreds. In the last chapter, in the section on counting, your child learned the words *ten, twenty, thirty, forty, fifty, sixty, seventy, eighty, ninety,* and *one hundred.* For "Pigs, Pens, and Pundreds" your child will need to know how to count by these "tens" names, from ten to one hundred, and back. He must know the sequence of these names, and if your child played that last counting game in chapter 4, this should be easy.

Next, your child needs to be able to count by hundreds. This is very simple, as it is the same as counting by ones, but you attach the word "hundred": *one hundred, two hundred, three hundred, four hundred, five hundred, six hundred, seven hundred, eight hundred, nine hundred,* and *ten hundred,* or what we call *one thousand.* No one really says "ten-hundred," but since we do say *eleven hundred, twelve hundred, thirteen hundred, fourteen hundred, fifteen hundred, sixteen hundred, seventeen hundred, eighteen hundred,* and *nineteen hundred,* then we figure it's okay to say *ten hundred,* and, if you wish, *twenty hundred,* or *two thousand.*

If your child is a little uncertain about counting by tens and hundreds, then go back and play that final game in the last chapter, and show him those number tables again, reinforcing the sequence of the tens numbers. Once he's got this reasonably mastered, he is ready for "Pigs, Pens, and Pundreds."

In this game we want to show you, eventually, how to teach your child to add 3-digit numbers together. But first, let's recapitulate. We started this chapter by adding up 1-digit numbers using the little pigs. When we add two 1-digit numbers and the answer comes out as a 2-digit number, we can use this sum to help your child understand what a 2-digit number actually is. Say we add 5 pigs to 6 pigs:

$$6 + 5 = 11$$

Your child won't know the answer to this problem without counting up to 11, or memorizing the addition table problem of 6 + 5, which we don't want your child to have to do just yet. He can learn to add without memorizing anything by playing "Pigs, Pens, and Pundreds."

So far, we've just shown you and your child individual pigs, like those on the following page. These are "loose" pigs, just running around in the field. Now we want to group some of them together into a *pen;* that is, a *pen of pigs.* How many pigs should we put into the pen? For reasons soon to be obvious, we will *always* put 10 pigs into a pen. On the page after the one with the loose pigs, we've presented a picture of a *pen of pigs*. There they are in their little pen. Show this to your child and tell him that they aren't loose pigs anymore, but now they are grouped together into a pen.

PIGS
Loose pigs for your child to cut out

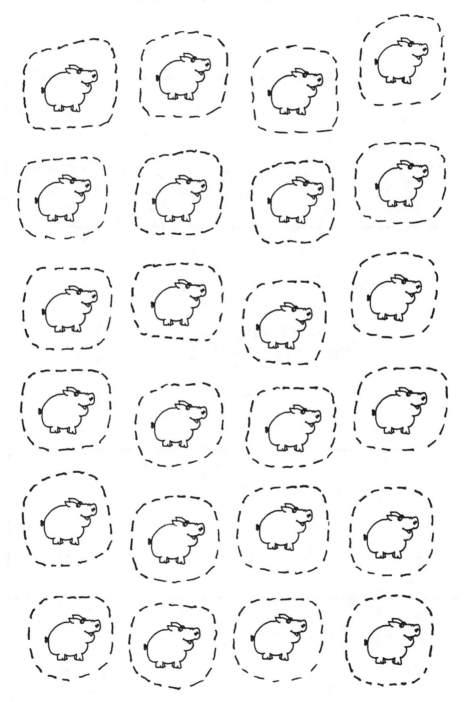

A PEN OF PIGS
Ten pigs in a pen

An Empty Pen
To Be Filled with Pigs

1	2	3	4	5
6	7	8	9	10

What we want you to do now is to photocopy the pen-of-pigs page once, along with the page of loose pigs once, and then turn to pages 72 and 73 and photocopy the "pundred of pigs" 22 times. Then have your child cut out all the loose pigs and place them on a table. Have her cut out each *pen of pigs* from two of the copies you made of the *pundred-of-pigs* page and place them on the table. Do not cut up the other 20 pundred-of-pigs pages (we will explain their use later). When you're finished, you'll have 38 loose pigs, 20 pens, and 20 "pundreds." Then we will be ready to play.*

Now let's do the 8 + 5 problem. Have your child count out 8 loose pigs and group them together, and then count out 5 loose pigs and group them together. Instead of just counting up *one, two, three, four, five, six, seven, eight, nine, ten, eleven, twelve, thirteen* to get the total, have your child group the loose pigs into a pen. Since there are 10 pigs in a pen, she will be able to make 1 pen of pigs, with 3 pigs left over. So:

8 + 5
or
8 pigs plus 5 pigs
equals 1 pen and 3 pigs.
1 pen and 3 pigs is the same as
13 loose pigs.
So 8 + 5 = 13

Let's try another one. Say we want to add 9 + 7. The answer, as you know, is 16. But your child doesn't know this, so you can show him with pigs. Have him count out 9 loose pigs and 7 loose pigs and group them into two separate piles. Then, bring these together into one pile of pigs. Next, as we just did, have your child regroup them into a pen. The answer, then, is 1 pen and 6 pigs left over, which would look like what we've pictured below:

---

*Be sure to SAVE all the loose pigs, pens, and pundreds in a safe place after playing these addition games. We will be using them for future games in subsequent chapters.

1 PEN OF PIGS

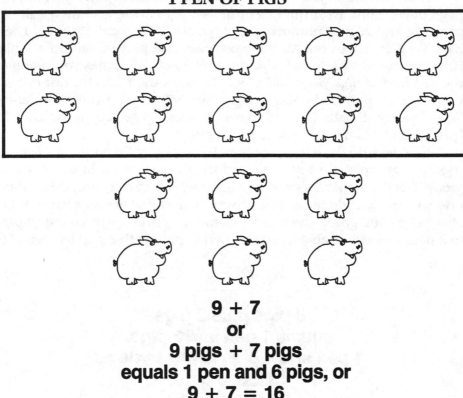

9 + 7
or
9 pigs + 7 pigs
equals 1 pen and 6 pigs, or
9 + 7 = 16

But what if we want to add 9 pigs to 13 pigs? Or 13 + 9 = ?

13 pigs = 10 pigs + 3 pigs, or 1 pen with 3 pigs left over. And, 9 pigs = 9 pigs.

Have your child figure this out by playing with the loose pigs and the pens. That is, lay out 13 loose pigs into one pile and 9 pigs into another pile; then have him regroup them into pens, as before. But this time, use the cutout of an *empty* pen. That is, when he collects a group of 10 loose pigs, have him place each loose pig into the empty pen on top of the numbers already there, one pig for each number.

As he will discover with this problem, he can make more than 1 pen. In fact, there will be 2 pens with 2 pigs left over. Since he already knows how to count by tens, he knows that *twenty* comes after *ten*, so you can remind him that the 2 pens equals 20 pigs, with 2 loose pigs left over. Then he has only to count two up from twenty, or *twenty-one, twenty-two.* So:

$$13 + 9 =$$
$$\textbf{2 pens} + \textbf{2 pigs} =$$
$$20 + 2 =$$
$$22$$

This problem is illustrated on the following page.

It might be a good idea, since we will be doing lots more of these problems, to help your child practice the conversion of large numbers into pens and pigs, until he automatically knows what makes up a number in terms of pens and pigs. First, we'll do just pens. Show your child this list and place the pens down on the table and have him count with you from 10 to 100:

1 pen = 10
2 pens = 20
3 pens = 30
4 pens = 40
5 pens = 50
6 pens = 60
7 pens = 70
8 pens = 80
9 pens = 90
10 pens = 100

Review these with your child. Then mix them up, putting different numbers of pens down on the table and have your child tell you how many pigs there are. For example, lay out 6 pens and ask your child to tell you how many pigs there are. He should now know that there are 60 pigs. Then have your child go the other direction. You give your child the number, and have him put the appropriate number of pens on the table. For example, you say " Show me 80 pigs," and he puts down 8 pens on the table. And so on. Practice in both directions until your child has mastered this skill.

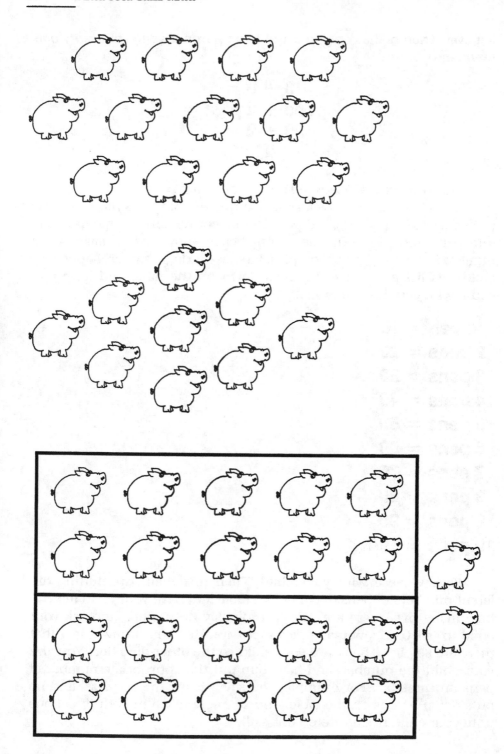

Now we'll make the game slightly more complex, but your child will master it easily because it follows simply from what we've just done. We have included loose pigs with the pens. Here are some numbers to practice with:

**28 pigs = 2 pens with 8 loose pigs,
or 20 pigs + 8 pigs.
36 pigs = 3 pens and 6 loose pigs.
45 pigs = 4 pens and 5 loose pigs.
53 pigs = 5 pens and 3 loose pigs.
67 pigs = 6 pens and 7 loose pigs.
79 pigs = 7 pens and 9 loose pigs.
82 pigs = 8 pens and 2 loose pigs.
50 pigs = 5 pens and no loose pigs.
91 pigs = 9 pens and 1 loose pig.
48 pigs = 4 pens and 8 loose pigs.**

Practice some more with your child, but this time have your child lay out pens and loose pigs for these equations:

14 pigs = ?	**84 pigs = ?**
98 pigs = ?	**48 pigs = ?**
31 pigs = ?	**17 pigs = ?**
76 pigs = ?	**63 pigs = ?**
19 pigs = ?	**51 pigs = ?**
28 pigs = ?	**45 pigs = ?**

Next, play the game backward. Present your child with actual pens and pigs on the table, and have your child tell you the number. For example, you lay out 4 pens and 3 pigs, and your child tells you there are 43 pigs. We don't need to give you examples here, as any combination of pens and pigs will do. Practice this game for as long as you need to until your child has mastered the concept of converting numbers into pens and pigs, and converting pens and pigs into numbers. Then doing the next set of addition games should be a breeze.

Now that your child understands this math game, have her try the following addition games, grouping the pens and pigs together on the table and coming up with the answer, as we just did. As you will quickly see, your child will need to use many pens and pigs, so be sure to have photocopied enough pens.

Since it is cumbersome to group together 23 loose pigs and 64 loose pigs (as in the second problem), this is the time to make the transition with your child to using just pens for the number in the tens column, and loose pigs for the number in the ones column. Your child knows how to do this because this is the game we just played of converting numbers to pens and pigs, and converting pens and pigs to numbers. So to do these addition games your child will first convert the numbers into pens and pigs, and then group those together and reconvert back into numbers.

For example, in the first problem below she will convert 12 into 1 pen and 2 pigs, and 15 into 1 pen and 5 pigs, for a total of 2 pens and 7 pigs, which is 27. In the second problem she will convert 23 into 2 pens and 3 pigs, and 64 into 6 pens and 4 pigs. She'll then regroup these (actually doing so on the table) into separate piles of 8 pens and 7 pigs, or 87.

12 + 15 = ?
23 + 64 = ?
23 + 36 = ?
42 + 47 = ?
73 + 16 = ?

Now consider the problem of adding

48 + 35

This is a special problem because after combining the two groups we have 7 pens and 13 loose pigs (4 pens and 8 pigs plus 3 pens and 5 pigs). Now we simplify the problem by converting the 13 loose pigs into 1 pen and 3 loose pigs. That gives us 8 pens and 3 loose pigs, or 83.

48 + 35 = 83

Whenever the math problem has 10 or more loose pigs left over, we should take 10 of those pigs and put them into a pen, and then combine that pen with the other pens in the problem. As a demonstration of this, we show how this might look, below:

48 pigs

35 pigs

48 + 35 = 83

A PUNDRED OF PIGS

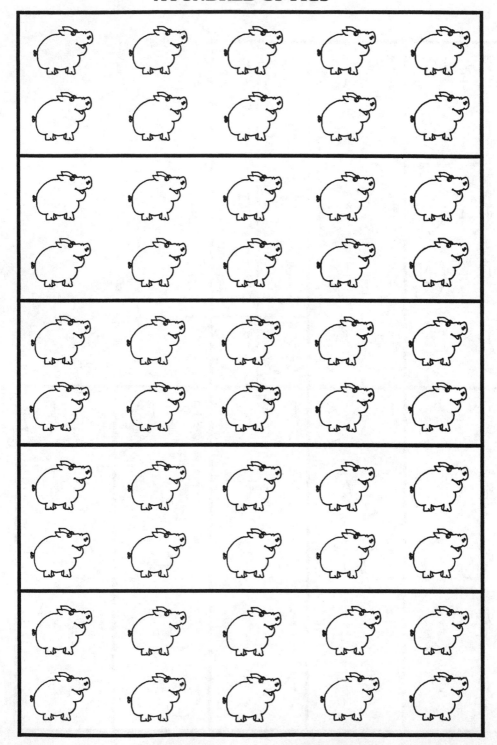

10 pens of pigs

Pundreds of Pigs

Thus far in this game, using pigs and pens, your child has been able to do any addition game to a hundred, because 10 pens equals 100 pigs. Some addition problems involve numbers that add up to a 3-digit number greater than a hundred. For these, we will now introduce the "pundred." A pundred is 100 pigs, or 10 pens. On the previous pages there's a picture of a pundred of pigs, which consists of 10 pens of pigs, and hence 100 pigs. You have already photocopied this page and now we will use it for the next game.

With this pundred of pigs (10 pigs in each of 10 pens) you can teach your child problems like 72 + 55. First, remind him that 72 pigs is 7 pens and 2 pigs, and that 55 pigs is 5 pens and 5 pigs. Then show him how 72 + 55 is 12 pens and 7 pigs. But because 10 pens make a pundred, we can simplify this answer to 1 pundred, 2 pens, and 7 pigs; hence, one hundred and twenty-seven pigs. Therefore,

$$72 + 55 = 127$$

Now let's try another problem:

$$93 + 47 = ?$$

With the loose pundreds, pens, and pigs, your child can group together 9 loose pens and 3 loose pigs; and then group together 4 loose pens and 7 loose pigs. Then, to do the addition problem, he can move to one side the 13 loose pens, and to the other side the 10 loose pigs—13 pens is 1 pundred and 3 pens, and 10 pigs is just 1 pen. Then we simplify again, combining the pens together, giving us 1 pundred and 4 pens, or one hundred and forty pigs altogether. Therefore:

$$93 + 47 = 140$$

The actual physical and visual process of moving around and grouping together pundreds, pens, and pigs should be a great way to get your child to conceptualize what actually is happening in the math game of addition. Once this concept is understood, the other functions of subtraction, multiplication, and division will come much more easily.

Now, you see, once you have taught your child that he can easily add 2-digit numbers together using this "10 pigs in 10 pens makes a pundred" game, you can take it as far as you like, but first we should practice recognition of the pundred numbers:

1 pundred = 100
2 pundreds = 200
3 pundreds = 300
4 pundreds = 400
5 pundreds = 500
6 pundreds = 600
7 pundreds = 700
8 pundreds = 800
9 pundreds = 900
10 pundreds = 1000
11 pundreds = 1100
12 pundreds = 1200
13 pundreds = 1300
14 pundreds = 1400
15 pundreds = 1500
16 pundreds = 1600
17 pundreds = 1700
18 pundreds = 1800
19 pundreds = 1900
20 pundreds = 2000

In the last chapter your child learned the names of these numbers, but it might be a good idea at this point to review them. Again, it is okay for now to use the term "ten-hundred" for 1000, and "twenty-hundred" for 2000, but eventually you will want to tell your child that we have different words for these—*one thousand* for 1000, and *two thousand* for 2000.

Next, your child should be able to give the name for a 3-digit number when you show her one on the table using pundreds, pens, and pigs, and vice versa. For example, show her these numbers in pundreds, pens, and pigs on the table and have her tell you the number, beginning with just pundreds, and then adding pens and pigs:

200
500
700
300
100
340
620
840
270
369
728
372
903
483

Now reverse the game, this time showing your child the number and having her show you what this looks like on the table using pundreds, pens, and pigs. Say to your child, "Show me 600 pigs"; "Show me 400 pigs;" and so on.

600
400
700
420
680
410
573
598
671

Now your child is ready for adding 3-digit numbers. Let's start with a simple one:

321 + 465

The first thing to do is have your child arrange the pundreds, pens, and pigs for the two numbers, using 3 pundreds, 2 pens, and 1 pig for the first number, and 4 pundreds, 6 pens, and 5 pigs for the second number. Then addition is easy. Bringing everything together gives us 7 pundreds, 8 pens, and 6 pigs. So:

321 + 465 = 786

Now let's try one slightly more difficult, this time with one "carry over" process.

419 + 278

As usual, have your child group the two numbers with the pundreds, pens, and pigs; then bring them together for a total of 6 pundreds, 8 pens, and 17 pigs. But here your child will see that she can do one more step, which she already knows from before. That is, 17 pigs is 1 pen and 7 pigs, so she can "carry over" the 1 pen and add it to the 8 pens, making a total of 9 pens, so the answer is 6 pundreds, 9 pens, 7 pigs, or

419 + 278 = 697

Now we'll try one with a double carry over:

264 + 379

Thus far we have been having your child add from left to right— that is, combining the pundreds first, then the pens, and finally the pigs. This time let's add from right to left, the way it is traditionally taught in school. Start by having your child collect the loose pigs (4 and 9), which fit into 1 pen, with 3 pigs left over. This gives us 1 new pen added to the 6 pens and 7 pens already there in the problem, giving us 14 pens. But 14 pens becomes 1 pundred and 4 pens. Adding the 1 new pundred to the 2 pundreds and 3 pundreds already there in the problem, gives us 6 pundreds.

6 pundreds, 4 pens, and 3 pigs, or
6 hundreds, 4 tens, and 3 ones, or
Six hundred and forty three, or

6 4 3

So:

264 + 379 = 643

The next 3-digit number addition problem represents one more step of difficulty, because the answer will be a 4-digit number. But it's just as easy as what we've been doing, and your child has already mastered all the skills needed to do it. Let's try:

826 + 733

You might, for fun, have your child do this problem both right to left and left to right, the second time having him check the first answer by a different means. From right to left, he will have 9 pigs, 5 pens, and 15 pundreds. And since there are no carry overs in this problem, it is really easy to reverse the process and go left to right: 15 pundreds, 5 pens, 9 pigs. But let's look at that answer. Instead of having a single-digit pundreds number, we've got a double-digit pundreds number (15). So the answer is:

15 pundred, 5 pens, 9 pigs, or
15 hundred and 59, or
1559, so
826 + 733 = 1559

Finally, we'll do one last one, this time with a triple carry over:

759 + 657

No sweat! Left to right or right to left (or both) will give your child the answer. If left to right, we bring the two numbers together to get 13 pundreds, 10 pens, and 16 pigs, but 10 pens is a pundred, and 16 pigs is a pen and 6 pigs, so we end up with 14 pundreds, 1 pen, 6 pigs, or

1416. Right to left gives us 16 pigs, 10 pens, and 13 pundreds, and your child can do the same combining and carrying over, giving the same answer of 1416.

$$759 + 657 = 1416$$

Summing Up

Let's see what you've taught your child so far. You've played addition games of adding up pictures of pigs; you've played addition games with both pigs *and* numbers, making the connection between the object and the symbol that it represents, together with teaching your child how to add 1-digit numbers. Then you moved up to adding 1-digit numbers that totaled a 2-digit number, and finally you graduated to adding a 1-digit to a 2-digit number, a 2-digit number to a 2-digit number, and even adding 3-digit numbers together, using the "Pigs, Pens, and Pundreds" game. Once your child grasped this game she could add any combination 1-, 2-, or 3-digit numbers together, either left to right or right to left, and do it either with pigs, pens, and pundreds, or with actual numbers on a page.

Math on Paper

There is one final thing left to do, and that is to practice these problems on paper. We need to teach your child how to do these addition problems with paper and pencil using just the numbers, and *not* using the pigs, pens, and pundreds. It might be a good idea to start with some easy 1-digit problems and work our way back up to 3-digit problems.

The first thing to show your child is that when we do math with paper and pencil we put the numbers down vertically instead of horizontally, with the plus (+) sign next to the bottom number. Then show your child how to put the answer down below the line. Be sure to remind him that we are really doing the same thing of bringing together two numbers into one, but when they are lined up vertically, they are lined up in columns that represent pigs, pens, and pundreds. So in the first problem below, your child will bring together, or add, 7 pigs and 2 pigs together, and write down the answer of 9 below the line.

In the case of 2-digit numbers, the number on the right represents the pigs, or ones, and the number on the left represents the pens, or tens. In a 3-digit number the number on the right is again pigs, or ones, the number in the middle is pens, or tens, and the number on the left is pundreds, or hundreds. Reinforce to your child that the order is always the same, from right to left it is pigs, pens, and pundreds. Your child already knows this from practicing the numbers earlier in this chapter, but it is a good idea to remind him when doing these problems.

Finally, we need to discuss how to teach your child "carrying over" in doing math problems on paper without pigs, pens, and pundreds. The principle, of course, is the same, but you need to show your child the process. Let's take something simple, like 15 + 8. We would write it thus:

$$
\begin{array}{r}
{}^{1}15 \\
+\ 8 \\
\hline
23
\end{array}
$$

Say to your child: "We do this problem the same way we did it with pigs and pens, but here we write down the numbers as we go. First, we bring together the loose pigs, or ones, of 5 and 8, which is 13. But remember that 13 is 1 pen and 3 pigs, so we *put down* the 3 pigs and *carry over* the pen. So we don't forget that we carried over the extra pen, we can put a little 1 above the big 1. Since 15 is 1 pen and 5 pigs, we add the extra pen to the 1 pen, giving us 2 pens, so we *put down* the 2 pens next to the 3 pigs, so the answer is 2 pens, 3 pigs, or 23."

The process is the same for adding a 2-digit number to another 2-digit number. For example, let's try 23 + 48:

$$
\begin{array}{r}
{}^{1}23 \\
+\ 48 \\
\hline
71
\end{array}
$$

Have your child proceed as before, combining the 3 and the 8, which gives 1 pig and 1 pen. Have him carry over the extra pen (don't forget to put a little 1 up next to the 2) to add to the 2 pens and 4 pens already there. And we end up with 7 pens and 1 pig, or 71.

Finally, to add a 3-digit number to another 3-digit number, the process is the same, but now we've got pundreds. For example: 278 + 467:

$$
\begin{array}{r}
{\scriptstyle 1\ 1} \\
278 \\
+\,467 \\
\hline
745
\end{array}
$$

As before, have your child add 8 + 7 to get 15. Put down the 5 and carry the 1, giving us 8 pens plus 6 pens, or 14. Put down the 4 and carry the 1, giving us 3 pundreds plus 4 pundreds, or 7 pundreds, 4 pens, 5 pigs, or 745.

Go through the problems below, working them with your child or, if he is ready, go ahead and let him work them himself. You and your child can check the answers, which appear on the page following the problems. If he is having a little trouble doing them just on paper, you can begin doing them with pigs, pens, and pundreds, and then go back and do the same problems with just the numbers which, since he has already worked them out, should be even easier. We've also included adding three numbers together of 1-, 2-, and 3-digits for a slightly greater challenge your child may enjoy.

① 7 +2

② 6 +3

③ 3 +1

④ 9 +1

⑤ 5 +4

⑥ 2 +5

⑦ 9 +2

⑧ 2 +9

⑨ 8 +4

⑩ 4 +7

⑪ 7 +9

⑫ 4 +5

⑬ 10 +2

⑭ 19 +4

⑮ 13 +8

⑯ 17 +7

⑰ 14 +9

⑱ 16 +5

⑲ 11 +9

⑳ 18 +4

㉑ 12 +9

㉒ 15 +7

㉓ 17 +3

㉔ 10 +6

㉕ 22 +73

㉖ 56 +92

㉗ 83 +35

㉘ 29 +21

㉙ 66 +66

㉚ 92 +34

(31)	(32)	(33)	(34)	(35)	(36)
36	74	99	58	27	82
+ 93	+ 29	+ 55	+ 38	+ 28	+ 61

(37)	(38)	(39)	(40)	(41)	(42)
12	21	19	35	88	11
+ 19	+ 75	+ 16	+ 29	+ 10	+ 52

(43)	(44)	(45)	(46)	(47)
395	264	118	254	285
+ 839	+ 132	+ 635	+ 522	+ 992

(48)	(49)	(50)	(51)	(52)
111	554	294	114	123
+ 352	+ 874	+ 223	+ 776	+ 333

(53)	(54)	(55)	(56)	(57)
725	543	203	100	199
+ 111	+ 790	+ 927	+ 101	+ 201

(58)	(59)	(60)	(61)	(62)	(63)	(64)
2	8	3	9	5	8	1
4	9	2	0	3	1	9
+ 7	+ 3	+ 6	+ 7	+ 2	+ 1	+ 8

(65)	(66)	(67)	(68)	(69)	(70)
84	23	11	66	53	72
22	45	17	87	10	78
+ 11	+ 28	+ 45	+ 23	+ 56	+ 12

(71)	(72)	(73)	(74)	(75)	(76)
572	672	113	201	781	445
211	900	222	659	221	556
+ 100	+ 334	+ 328	+ 376	+ 300	+ 144

Answers

1.	9	2.	9	3.	4	4.	10	5.	9
6.	7	7.	11	8.	11	9.	12	10.	11
11.	16	12.	9	13.	12	14.	23	15.	21
16.	24	17.	23	18.	21	19.	20	20.	22
21.	21	22.	22	23.	20	24.	16	25.	95
26.	148	27.	118	28.	50	29.	132	30.	126
31.	129	32.	103	33.	154	34.	96	35.	55
36.	143	37.	31	38.	96	39.	35	40.	64
41.	98	42.	63	43.	1234	44.	396	45.	753
46.	776	47.	1277	48.	463	49.	1428	50.	517
51.	890	52.	456	53.	836	54.	1333	55.	1130
56.	201	57.	400	58.	13	59.	20	60.	11
61.	16	62.	10	63.	10	64.	18	65.	117
66.	96	67.	73	68.	176	69.	119	70.	162
71.	883	72.	1906	73.	663	74.	1236	75.	1302
76.	1145								

Congratulations to you and your child! You have mastered the skills of addition. This was no easy task, and it sets the stage for all the other math skills, including subtraction, multiplication, and division, making them easier to learn. We believe that this system of teaching your child math is useful because it is like a game, which is fun, it is hands-on, so math becomes something real and physical, you can add left to right or right to left and, finally, it gives children a feeling of power to have learned all this without having to memorize anything. Just think. Your young child, even knowing nothing at all about math, can, at this point, add 3-digit numbers that are intimidating even for many adults. We hope this will make your child excited about math.

Now, let's go on to subtraction in the next chapter which, with all the math skills your child now has, will be relatively simple, and just as much fun!

CHAPTER

6

What's the Difference?
Subtraction Games

Remember the "Let's Measure Cookies" game you played with your child? How many cookies were left over from the batch you made by the time you got to chapter 5, the addition chapter? (Probably none, but never mind—they were good cookies.)

If you recall, the addition problem we started with in chapter 5 was that you had three cookies and your child had four cookies, for a total of seven cookies. If you followed directions, there should have been 4-1/2 dozen cookies, a total of 54 cookies, or 5 tens and 4 ones. You and your child ate 7 cookies. How many were left can be another math game for you to play with your child—this one called "subtraction."

In the game of addition we were *bringing together* two sets of numbers, such as 4 cookies and 3 cookies. In the game of subtraction we will be *taking away* one number from another number. Now that your child knows addition and is familiar with the concept of performing an operation with two numbers, learning subtraction will be relatively easy. You will teach your child to *take away* one number from a larger number (up to 3-digit numbers) without having to memorize any math tables!

Let's start the subtraction cookie game with an easy problem, taking the 7 cookies you and your child ate away from a total of 10. So the subtraction cookie game is 10 − 7. If you have some cookies there in front of you, have your child actually take them away. If not, use a copy of the illustration of cookies, below, having your child cross out 7 cookies. Then ask her: "How many cookies are left after we eat 7?"

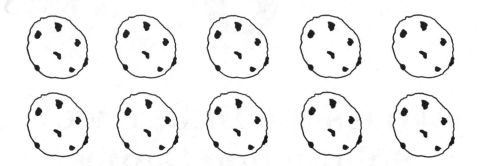

Now your child can see that:

10 cookies − 7 cookies = 3 cookies

Learning the game of subtraction follows most directly and appropriately after learning the game of addition. Though our semantic habits have us rank these arithmetical functions as *addition, subtraction, multiplication,* and *division,* we must not let this blind us to the fact that this ranking is *not* one of importance. All four functions of arithmetic are equally important in dealing with the world. Subtraction is one of the four basic rules of numbers. These rules, or operations, are the first things we do with numbers, and the rule of subtraction is what we will focus on in this chapter.

First we need to introduce your child to the terminology of subtraction. When we subtract, we are *taking away from,* and the difference is what is *left over* after we have subtracted. So in the above problem we *subtracted* 7 cookies from 10 cookies and got a **difference** of 3 cookies.

Pigs in a Pen Again

Let's try another subtraction game, this time using the old familiar pigs-in-a-pen game, beginning with a group of 8 pigs. Start by asking your child how many pigs there are in the group of pigs shown below. She will count 8.

Next, have her *subtract* 3 pigs from those 8 pigs, that is:

8 – 3

You can have your child perform the subtraction problem by having her cover up 3 pigs with her hand. It would be even better, however, to take out the pigs, pens, and pundreds (which you used in the addition games) and put 8 loose pigs on the table in front of you and have her literally *take away* 3 pigs. Then she can perform the subtraction problem manually and actually see that there are 5 pigs left over, or a difference of 5. Ask her: "How many pigs are left?" Then show her that the full subtraction problem looks like this:

8 – 3 = 5

Let's try another pig subtraction game. Show your child the 9 pigs below and give her this problem:

9 – 4

She can figure out this problem the same way, by taking away 4 of the 9 pigs and seeing there are 5 pigs left. So:

$$9 - 4 = 5$$

You can see from this that subtraction is related to addition because we can reverse this game. There are 5 pigs left on the table. Now have your child *add* 4 pigs to these 5 and tell you what the total number of pigs is. She will get a total of 9 pigs:

$$9 - 4 = 5$$
and
$$5 + 4 = 9$$

Let's try some more of these subtraction games, taking away a 1-digit number from another 1-digit number, using the loose pigs.

$$4 - 3 = ?$$
$$7 - 5 = ?$$
$$3 - 1 = ?$$
$$8 - 6 = ?$$
$$6 - 5 = ?$$
$$9 - 2 = ?$$
$$2 - 1 = ?$$

5 − 2 = ?
9 − 7 = ?
8 − 2 = ?

There's Nothing to It!

Here's another subtraction twist: what happens if we take away *all* of the items from the total? That is, what is the answer when we subtract the total from the total? For example, what is the answer to this subtraction game?

$$5 - 5 = ?$$

The answer, of course, is "zero." What is zero? Zero = 0. This is an interesting symbol, isn't it, because it is a circle with *nothing* in it! The zero, to our knowledge, was first used in the seventh century in the Far East and had the shape of a "goose-egg," to designate a number place that represented nothing.

You can tell your child: "Okay, now we are going to learn something new about numbers. This something is nothing! Let's see how it works. If you have 5 cookies and you eat 5 cookies, how many cookies will you have left over? [Child says 'none'; if not, you say 'none.']

"Very good. Now, how can we write out 'none'? Let's draw a circle with nothing in it. [Draw the circle.] Look! See what's inside this circle? *Nothing* is inside the circle. So this circle represents nothing. We call this nothing a *zero*. It looks like this. [Draw another circle.] Now you draw one. [Have your child draw a circle.]"

It's time to visualize the zero concept with some zero subtraction games:

If we take 3 pigs away from 3 pigs, how many are left?

6 pigs *minus* 6 pigs = ? pigs:

You can also reverse the zero game by *adding* a set of objects to nothing and getting the same number. For example, 5 pigs + 0 pigs = 5 pigs. Explain to your child that adding nothing to something always equals the same number you began with because the zero represents nothing—8 pigs + 0 pigs = 8 pigs. And so forth.

You can practice the zero game with any object from around the house, for example:

5 forks − 5 forks = ? forks.

6 pencils + 0 pencils = ? pencils.

3 cups − 3 cups = ? cups.

8 pennies + 0 pennies = ? pennies.

7 spoons − 7 spoons = ? spoons.

2 pillows + 0 pillows = ? pillows.

More Pigs in a Pen

Now it's time to move on to a little harder type of subtraction problem—that is, subtracting numbers larger than one digit; for example, subtracting 2-digit numbers and 3-digit numbers from each other. Since this will require *borrowing* numbers, and working in sets of ones, tens, and hundreds, we will return to our trusty pigs, pens, and pundreds, this time with subtraction.

Remember, the game of subtraction is played the same way as the game of addition, because, as we have seen, subtraction and addition are related. So let's start with 13 pigs and *take away*, or *subtract*, 5 pigs. Remind your child that a pen consists of ten pigs. Here's what the problem looks like so you can show your child.

This scattered mess of pigs, of course, probably doesn't look like a subtraction problem to either you or your child, but one quick way to show her how subtraction works is to have her cover up 5 of the 13 pigs (there's a group of 5 on the left), and ask her how many remain that are not covered up. The answer is 8, of course, showing her that:

$$13 - 5 = 8$$

Or, even better, use 13 loose pigs and have your child literally *take away*, or *subtract*, 5 of the loose pigs from a pile of 13 loose pigs and ask her how many are left over. That is, the *difference* will be 8. But now let's see how this will work if the pigs are grouped into a *pen* of pigs. Have your child put 10 of the 13 loose pigs into a pen. Now you will have a pen of 10 loose pigs, and 3 loose pigs by themselves, like this:

Since there is 1 pen and 3 loose pigs, and we want to subtract 5 loose pigs from the total, here you can teach your child about *borrowing*, or taking away, some pigs from the pen. Since we have 3 loose pigs and we want to subtract 5 pigs altogether, we need to borrow, or take, 2 pigs from the pen. These 2 pigs, added to the 3 loose pigs, makes 5 loose pigs. Now your child can see the 8 loose pigs left in the pen. In this case, the pen will need to be a broken one so that your child *can* physically remove 2 loose pigs. So:

13 − 5 = 8

You might help her with this concept by suggesting that she "let the pigs out of their pen" by trading the pen in for 10 loose pigs. The point, of course, is to get your child to grasp the concept of "breaking up" the pen for pigs, or the 10 for ones. After your child has done this, do a similar problem, but this time start with a solid pen and loose pigs. We'll make the problem 15 − 9, so put 1 pen and 5 loose pigs down on the table and show your child this problem:

15 − 9

Your child may see that she can't take away 9 pigs from the 5 loose pigs, so she will need to trade in the pen for 10 loose pigs, and then take away the 9.

Let's practice some more of these, using the pigs and pens on a table for the following subtraction problems:

17 − 8 = ?
13 − 6 = ?
16 − 9 = ?
12 − 4 = ?
18 − 9 = ?
11 − 2 = ?
15 − 8 = ?
14 − 6 = ?
13 − 9 = ?
17 − 9 = ?

Let's try a larger pigs-in-a-pen subtraction game, this time subtracting 22 pigs from 35 pigs. First remind her that 35 pigs is 3 pens and 5 pigs, and that 22 pigs is 2 pens and 2 pigs.

Start, as we did with the addition problems, by having your child group the loose pens ("loose" because you've broken up a pundred to get them) and pigs on a table, but this time she just needs to group 35, or 3 pens and 5 pigs. Then have her *take away* 22 pigs, or 2 pens and 2 pigs.

Now show her that when she *takes away* 2 pens from 3 pens it leaves 1 pen, and that when she *takes away* 2 pigs from 5 pigs it leaves 3 pigs, so the *difference* is (=) 1 pen and 3 pigs, or 13 pigs. We've illustrated this for you on the following page:

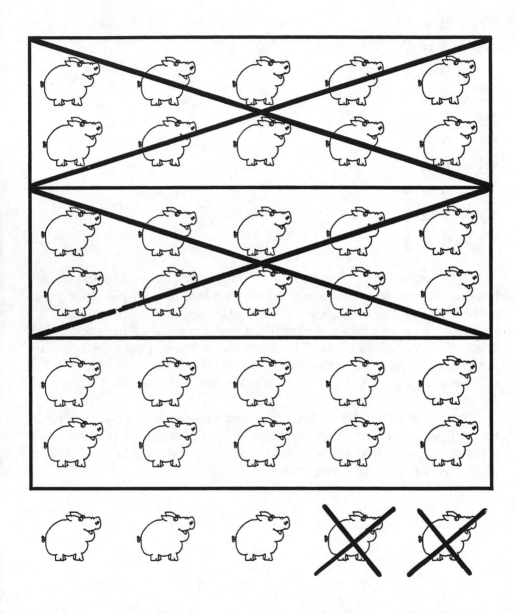

35 − 22 = 1 pen, 3 pigs
35 − 22 = 13

Here's another pigs-in-a-pen subtraction game. This one is a little more complicated, as you will have your child subtract 37 from 85. Start by having your child lay out 85 pigs on the table. He should automatically pull out 8 pens and 5 pigs, but let's begin this more complicated problem by helping him a bit and making one of those 8 pens a broken pen so that he can easily remove 2 loose pigs from it. We've demonstrated this on the next page, showing how your child can do this with the broken pen.

He will begin subtracting 7 by taking away the 5 loose pigs and then going to the broken pen to take away 2 more pigs. Then he can take away 3 pens from the 7 solid pens left on the table, leaving 4 pens and 8 loose pigs. See how easy it is? Therefore:

$$85 - 37 = 48$$

85 − 37 = 4 pens, 8 pigs
85 − 37 = 48.

Let's try another, this time subtracting 65 from 92.

$$92 - 65 = ?$$

Start with 9 pens and 2 pigs, but make one of these pens a pen of 10 loose pigs. We also want to demonstrate in this problem that your child can subtract from left to right just as easily as he can from right to left. With one of the pens fractured into 10 loose pigs, it will be easy for him, going from left to right, to take away 6 pens from the 9 pens, leaving 3 pens, one of which should be the fractured pen. Then he merely takes away 5 pigs, 3 of which will come from the fractured pen, leaving 2 full pens and 7 loose pigs, or a subtraction answer of 27 pigs.

Next, you might try doing this problem with 9 solid pens and 2 loose pigs. As before, he'll remove 6 pens from 9 pens, leaving 3 pens and 2 pigs. But now he has to subtract 5 more loose pigs from this group, and there are only 2 of them there. What is needed are more loose pigs. So have your child exchange the solid pen for 10 loose pigs. Now he has 12 loose pigs from which he can take 5 away.

In addition to having him arrange the pigs and pens on the table, have him write the subtraction problem on a piece of paper to reinforce the connection between the fictional game of "Pigs, Pens, and Pundreds" and the real game of *ones, tens, and hundreds* which, of course, is our goal in playing this game in the first place. We don't think it is necessary that you explain this connection to your child. We feel that he will grasp the concept just by playing the games. Try some more of these subtraction problems in which your child must borrow pigs from a pen:

$$27 - 19 = ?$$
$$42 - 38 = ?$$
$$35 - 29 = ?$$
$$87 - 38 = ?$$
$$61 - 34 = ?$$
$$53 - 47 = ?$$
$$24 - 17 = ?$$
$$76 - 58 = ?$$
$$36 - 19 = ?$$
$$83 - 48 = ?$$

Subtracting 3-digit numbers involves the same process as subtracting 2-digit numbers but just requires an additional step of subtraction. For example, let's try an easy one like 574 − 342 = ? First, have your child write the problem on a sheet of paper, and then arrange her pens and pigs on the table into 5 pundreds, 7 pens, and 4 pigs. Then direct her to solve the problem by *subtracting*, or *taking away*, 3 pundreds, 4 pens, and 2 pigs. This one requires no breaking up of another pen or pundred, so she can easily take 3 pundreds from 5 pundreds, 4 pens from 7 pens, and 2 pigs from 4 pigs, to arrive at:

$$574 - 342 = 232$$

Practice several of these:

426 − 314 = ?
783 − 362 = ?
275 − 134 = ?
639 − 426 = ?
954 − 421 = ?
547 − 334 = ?
246 − 123 = ?
883 − 412 = ?
672 − 351 = ?
479 − 256 = ?

But now let's do some 3-digit problems that require *borrowing* from pens and pundreds to work them out.

We'll begin with:

$$256 - 138$$

Have your child group 2 pundreds, 5 pens, and 6 pigs on the table. Then let her try the problem herself, without your immediate help, to see if she can transfer the skills from the last set of 2-digit borrowing problems. Remind her, if necessary, that she will have to break up a pen in order to get enough pigs to take away 8 loose pigs. Then she subtracts the 3 pens from the 4 pens, leaving 1 pen. Finally, she will take away 1 pundred from the 2 pundreds, leaving a grand total of 1 pundred, 1 pen, and 8 pigs left over, so:

$$256 - 138 = 118$$

Let's practice a set of these 3-digit subtraction problems that require borrowing a pen using, as usual, the pigs, pens, and pundreds on the table:

426 − 219 = ?
683 − 348 = ?
825 − 718 = ?
368 − 139 = ?
937 − 619 = ?
342 − 127 = ?
267 − 149 = ?
783 − 546 = ?
453 − 238 = ?
658 − 239 = ?

Because these are a little more difficult, and your child may need to or want to practice more now or later, we've included 10 more subtraction problems with a single borrowing process:

742 − 328 = ?
537 − 129 = ?
845 − 717 = ?
458 − 149 = ?
574 − 326 = ?
685 − 568 = ?
978 − 869 = ?
365 − 289 = ?
395 − 118 = ?
752 − 547 = ?

Finally in this sequence we'll do some 3-digit subtraction problems that require breaking up both pens and pundreds.

We'll start with:

$$467 - 289$$

Again, just give her the problem and see if she can work it out herself. If she can, that's great, and you should be sure to praise her. If she needs a little guidance, remind her that, to begin, she will break up 1 pen of the 6 into 10 loose pigs, in order to get enough loose pigs, leaving (after taking away 9 loose pigs) 4 pundreds, 5 pens, and 8 pigs. But she won't be able to take 8 pens from 5 pens, so she will need to break up one of the 4 pundreds into 10 loose pens, leaving 3 pundreds, 7 pens, and 8 pigs. Finally, she takes 2 pundreds away from the 3 pundreds, leaving a grand total of 1 pundred, 7 pens, and 8 pigs:

$$467 - 289 = 178$$

Here are 10 more 3-digit subtraction problems that require borrowing both pundreds and pens:

$$736 - 569 = ?$$
$$378 - 199 = ?$$
$$543 - 268 = ?$$
$$656 - 397 = ?$$
$$483 - 195 = ?$$
$$375 - 286 = ?$$
$$835 - 247 = ?$$
$$483 - 395 = ?$$
$$284 - 196 = ?$$
$$647 - 368 = ?$$

Once again, for additional practice now or later, here are some more subtraction problems that require double borrowing:

$$553 - 367 = ?$$
$$735 - 298 = ?$$

$$421 - 249 = ?$$
$$538 - 369 = ?$$
$$356 - 278 = ?$$
$$958 - 769 = ?$$
$$885 - 698 = ?$$
$$741 - 568 = ?$$
$$648 - 459 = ?$$
$$888 - 699 = ?$$

Pennies, Dimes, and Dollars

Now that your child has mastered, or at least been introduced to, subtraction problems of various sorts, we can try another subtraction game that will reinforce the same principles of ones, tens, and hundreds that we've just been working with, as well as teach him the exchange value of money—that is, how many pennies make a dime, and how many dimes make a dollar. As you will see, the "Pigs, Pens, and Pundreds" game corresponds nicely to the "Pennies, Dimes, and Dollars" game we will now play. For starters, show your child the layout of pennies and dimes below and tell him:

"Good. Now that we understand how pigs, pens, and pundreds work in both addition and subtraction problems, and you know that pigs, pens, and pundreds are the same as ones, tens, and hundreds, we can play some math games with money. The way the game works is this: *pennies* are like pigs, *dimes* are like pens, and *dollars* are like pundreds. And they work the same way. See, 10 pennies is like 10 pigs. And just as we put the pigs in a pen to represent 10 pigs, we say that a dime represents 10 pennies. So a dime is 10 pennies. And what do you think a dollar is? That's right, a dollar is like a pundred, so a dollar is a hundred pennies, or 10 dimes."

Point out to your child that the rules of addition and subtraction in this game are the same as the ones in the pigs-in-a-pen game. That is, we can add or subtract both the ones column and the tens column to get our totals, whether we're adding or subtracting. For example, you can show your child that 7 pennies plus 6 pennies is 13 pennies, but it is also 1 dime with 3 pennies left over.

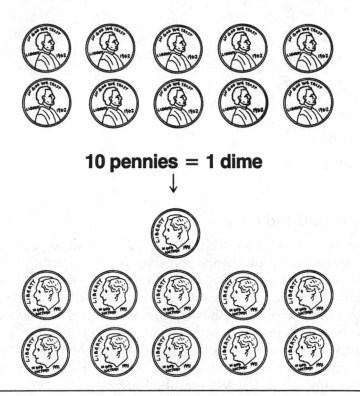

10 pennies = 1 dime
↓

10 dimes = 1 dollar
↓

Likewise, saying 13 pigs + 9 pigs = 22 pigs (or 2 pens and 2 pigs) is the same as saying that 13 pennies + 9 pennies = 22 pennies (or 2 dimes and 2 pennies). We think it might be a good idea to do both addition and subtraction problems with money, and now that your child can do both with the "Pigs, Pens, and Pundreds" game, this is a good way to wrap up both addition and subtraction. You'll need a roll of pennies, a roll of dimes, and 20 one-dollar bills. (For the bills you might want to use play money, from a Monopoly game, for instance.)

What we'd like you to do is turn back to the addition chapter, and work all those problems again with your child, from the beginning to the end, but this time use pennies, dimes, and dollars. For the more difficult 3-digit problems, such as adding 239 pennies to 364 pennies, remind your child that it's the same game—just with different names. So, to add 239 + 364, your child will collect the loose pennies of 9 and 4 and add them together, giving 13 pennies, or 3 pennies and 1 dime to be *carried over* to the dimes (tens) column. He can now add 1 + 3 + 6 to get 10 dimes. But 10 dimes is a *dollar*, so your child puts down the 0 and carries over the 1 dollar to the dollar column, and then adds 1 + 2 + 3 = 6. You can walk your child through this problem and get an answer of 6 dollars, 0 dimes and 3 pennies, or 239 + 364 = 603.

Now let's reverse these addition games into subtraction games, using the pennies, dimes, and dollars. It should be easy for your child to do a subtraction problem like 37 pennies minus 4 pennies, because he just has to subtract 4 from 7, leaving 33 pennies. But have him try 32 − 4. Once again, as he did earlier, he will find it necessary to break up the tens column (or dimes column) in order to "make change" for the problem. So remind your child that 32 is actually 3 dimes and 2 pennies. So if he "breaks up" a dime and moves the 10 pennies to the pennies column, he will have 2 dimes and 12 pennies. Now he can subtract 4 pennies from 12 pennies, leaving 8 pennies, and, since there are 2 dimes left, the answer to 32 − 4 is (=) 28 pennies, or 2 dimes, 8 pennies. Now go back to the beginning of this chapter, and rework all the subtraction problems from 1-digit to 3-digit problems, but this time use pennies, dimes, and dollars. A 3-digit problem, say 726 − 438, may seem hard to your child, but by now he should be ready and confident enough to handle these large numbers. Walk him through the problems the same way you did before with the pigs, pens, and pundreds, by having him break up the dimes or dollars as needed.

A Special Note on Encouragement

What do you do if your child doesn't get the right answer to the problems you've been practicing? This is an important subject that may come up at any point in the process of teaching your child math. First, you must be *positive*, not negative. Perhaps instead of saying, "You're wrong," say, "That's very creative, but not quite right, so let's look at it again and try another answer."

Praise is equally important. Your child will blossom and be eager to go on and learn more if your game playing is sprinkled with laudatory words—Good for you! Excellent! You're a little math whiz! I'm so proud of you!, and so on.

We have structured this book so that if your child doesn't understand something at any point along the way, you need only go back one step and run through it again. We recognize, of course, that there will be wide individual differences among children in how fast they grasp these basic math concepts, but if you start from the beginning and work (play) your way through the various games, your child should arrive at the end having learned all the math skills in this book. But there will be stumbling blocks for all children, so you need to be patient and positive. Once children have mastered subtraction, they will be halfway through the four basic rules of arithmetic, and will be ready to play multiplication!

CHAPTER

7

How Many Times? Multiplication Games

As a special reward for your child, who has been doing so well in learning the games of math, let's say you have purchased a box of candy to be devoured at the end of a subtraction session. "Congratulations," you tell your child, "you're doing great so far." But before you and your child take even one piece from that box, take a look at the layout of the candy. Notice how the candies are all lined up in rows. (Make sure the box of candy you buy is laid out this way.) Let's say there are 4 rows of candy, with 8 candies in each row. Here's your chance to teach your child another math skill—not addition, but a special form of fast addition called "multiplication." The question to ask your child is: "How many candies are there in this box?"

Initially this sounds like an addition game—4 rows with 8 candies in each row sounds like adding up 8 four times: 8 + 8 + 8 + 8. And really, that's exactly what it is. But the key word here is "times." How many *times* you add a number can be phrased another way. That is, how many *times* you add a number is the same as *multiplying* a number *times* another number. So our candy problem of adding 8 + 8 + 8 + 8 is the same as adding 8 four times, or 8 times 4, also written 8 × 4. When we use the word "times," it is not an addition problem but a multiplication problem.

Remember in the addition games when you helped your child

make the transition from counting to addition by showing him that the answer to What is 6 + 1? was the same as the answer to What number comes after 6? The answer to both was 7. Well, now that your child knows how to add, he can take the next step and play the multiplication game.

Say to your child, "The candy game of adding up 8 four times (8 + 8 + 8 + 8) sounds like saying we are adding 8, four *times*. Another way to say that is *8 times 4*. So 8 + 8 + 8 + 8 is the same as 8 times 4. Remember in addition we had a special symbol for the word "add" that was the + sign? Well, we have a special symbol for the word "times." It's an ×. So 8 + 8 + 8 + 8 is the same as writing 8 × 4, which we say is 8 times 4. This new game we are playing is called 'multiplication.' What we are doing is multiplying 8 times 4. So just as 8 + 8 + 8 + 8 = 32, so too does 8 × 4 = 32. They are really the same, but multiplication, once you learn how to do it, is a lot faster."

To reinforce this concept, try a bunch of different addition problems, like this one: Take 3 plates of cookies with 5 cookies on each plate, show them to your child, and ask: "How many cookies are there in all?"

Explain to your child, in the way we just did above, that the addition game for this would be 5 + 5 + 5, for a total of 15 cookies. Another way of saying 5 + 5 + 5 is to say 5, 3 *times*. The way we say this is, however, not 5, 3 times, but 5 times 3, or 5 × 3.

Similarly, 9 × 3 is like writing down 9 three times, which is the same as adding 9 + 9 + 9 which, because he can add, your child knows is 27. So 9 + 9 + 9 = 27 is the same as 9 × 3 = 27.

We can also play this game backward to reinforce the point. That is, ask your child: "5 × 3 is the same as what addition problem?" The answer, of course, is 5 + 5 + 5.

Now, go back to the problem 8 × 4, above. Say to your child, "8 × 4 is the same as what addition problem?" This, he may recall, was 8 + 8 + 8. Do a lot of these types of problems backward with your child. Then do them forward and backward, showing how addition and multiplication are similar to each other.

The important thing to teach your child at this point is the *concept* of multiplication. We are more interested in your child's learning what 8 × 4 *means* than in his learning what 8 × 4 *is*. Any calculator will tell you and your child what 8 × 4 is. What 8 × 4 *means* is a much deeper and more important concept.

So, what does 8 × 4 mean? It means the number of *times* we write down 8. In this problem we write down 8, 4 times, or 8 times 4, or 8 × 4. The key concept, then, is *times*. This is what turns addition into multiplication.

Before we go into games of multiplication that are more visual, it is important to set forth the terms used in multiplication games. In the above problem, 8 and 4 are the "multipliers," or the numbers to be *multiplied*. The symbol "×" tells us that a number is being multiplied "times" another number. So "×" and "times" designate the same function. The answer, or the final result of the problem, is called the "product." So the product of the multiplier 8 times the multiplier 4 = (equals) 32. You might show your child this illustration.

$$\begin{array}{r} \textbf{8} \quad \textit{multiplier} \\ \textit{times} \ \underline{\times\, \textbf{4}} \quad \textit{multiplier} \\ \textit{equals} \ \ \textbf{32} \quad \textit{product} \end{array}$$

Let's show your child another visual demonstration of the similarity between addition and multiplication. Then he can see how multiplication will enable him to find the total of a long addition problem in a similar but different and faster way. Let's start by arranging a rectangle of coins in a 4 by 2 or 2 by 4 rectangle.

In the first rectangle of coins we have a set of 4 coins, 2 times, so we can say that 4 times 2 equals 8.

In the second rectangle of coins we have a set of 2 coins, 4 times, so we can say that 2 times 4 equals 8.

This is called the *commutative* property of multiplication where the multipliers can be exchanged for each other without affecting the outcome of the problem. It doesn't matter what order we put the multipliers in, the answer is the same. So 4 × 2 is the same as 2 × 4. The numbers 4 and 2 can be switched around without affecting the product of (the answer to) the problem, 8.

We can do the same with a 4 by 3 rectangle, where 4 coins in 3 rows can be multiplied. So instead of adding 4 + 4 + 4, we reduce the problem to one of multiplying 4 × 3. The figures below visually demonstrate why 4 × 3 is the same as 4 + 4 + 4; and in the second 3 by 4 rectangle, where 3 coins in 4 rows can be multiplied, we can see why 3 × 4 is the same as 3 + 3 + 3 + 3.

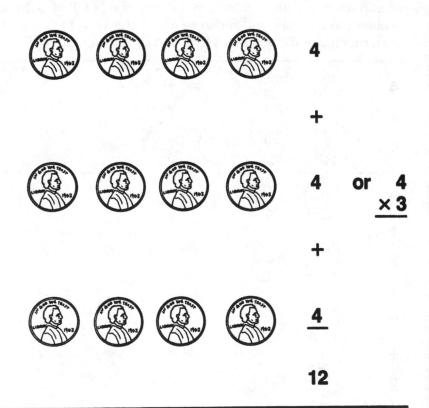

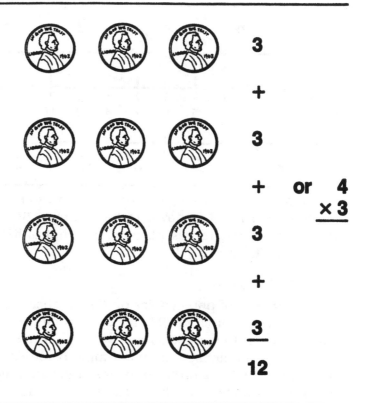

Another way to visualize this relationship between addition and multiplication can be seen in the number line below. Once again you can show your child why 6 × 2 = 12 is the same as 2 + 2 + 2 + 2 + 2 + 2 = 12, and why 6 × 2 is the same as 2 × 6.

Basically, what the number line does is present a visual display of the *additive* or *multiplicative* nature of numbers. That is, it shows your child that she can compare the math functions of addition and multiplication.

Tell your child: "If we look at the addition problem on the bottom of the number line we can see that 2 + 2 + 2 + 2 + 2 + 2 = 12. And when we look at the top of the line, we can see that this is the same thing as multiplying 6 times 2 or 2 times 6. That is, 2 chunks of 6 numbers is the same thing as 6 chunks of 2 numbers. Therefore, 6 × 2 = 12, and 2 × 6 = 12. Both of these are the same as the addition problem, except we are multiplying the numbers instead of adding them."

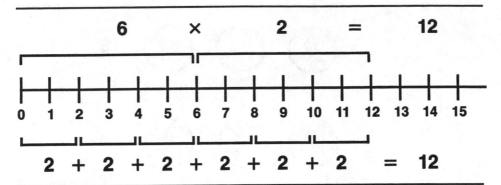

Another visual example of the relationship between addition and multiplication can be shown in the Number Box on the next page, where each square represents a number, not unlike the rectangles we formed with the coins.

The Squares Game

Make a number of photocopies of the Number Box on the next page, and then have your child fill in the appropriate boxes (with a crayon or marker pen) for the problems shown on the next page.

As we've demonstrated in a sample below, the 4×3 problem is the same as the 6×2 problem because they both require that we color in 12 squares. So both $4 \times 3 = 12$ and $6 \times 2 = 12$.

Not only that, you can get the product 12 by multiplying 12×1 or 1×12; 6×2 or 2×6; 4×3 or 3×4. Just think of that!

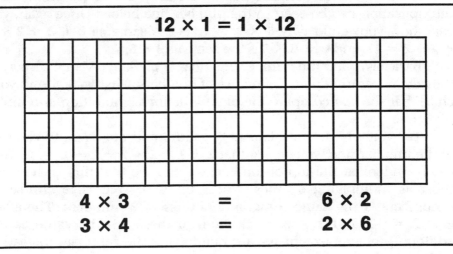

Using the photocopies you made of this page, have your child mark an X in the boxes (or color them in) that represent each problem. We've done one sample problem, 2 × 4, for you. Check the answers by counting squares.

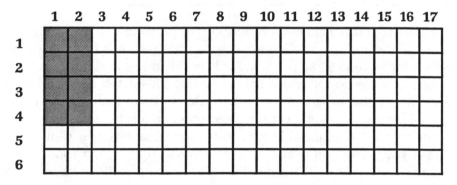

$$
\begin{array}{cccc}
8 & 3 & 2 & 4 \\
\times 2 & \times 3 & \times 5 & \times 5 \\
\hline
16 & 9 & 10 & 20 \\
\end{array}
$$

Number Box

Now have your child mark X's or color in the squares for the following problems. These problems are in reverse of just writing out the multiplication problem, and are meant to help your child learn what the process of multiplication actually means:

1. Mark 15 squares in 3 rows. (Answer: 5 × 3)
2. Mark 18 squares in 2 rows. (Answer: 9 × 2)
3. How many squares are in 2 × 4? (Answer: 8)
4. How can you mark 28 squares? (Answer: 7 × 4)
5. How many squares are in 17 × 1? (Answer: 17)
6. How can you mark 25 squares? (Answer: 5 × 5)

Much Ado About Nothing

With the squares game you just played you can also teach your child about zeros in multiplication by first telling him that anything multiplied by 0 will always be 0, and then showing him why this must be.

You can do this using the coloring game again and asking: "How many squares are in row 0?" Since your child will quickly see that there is no "row 0," the answer must be 0 (which means zero, or none). So $17 \times 0 = 0$. And $0 \times 5 = 0$. And so on.

Let's try some more multiplication problems using the squares game, to see how all of the principles you've been teaching your child come together. Have your child write in the answers for these problems:

3	4	2	6	10	5	4	7
$\times 2$	$\times 3$	$\times 2$	$\times 0$	$\times 1$	$\times 3$	$\times 5$	$\times 0$

Let's make this process a little more applicable to your child, this time using your child's allowance as a math game. Let's say your child's allowance is $5.00 a week. And let's also say that there is a toy he wants to save up for. Since this toy costs $40.00, tell him he'll have to save his allowance for 8 weeks in order to have enough money to buy it. Since he will likely want to know how much he will have saved over the 8 weeks, this should be a most interesting game for him.

Ask your child: "If you get $5.00 a week, how much money will you have in 8 weeks?" (If your child's allowance is a different amount, use your own figures.) Have your child fill in the squares in the number box we used previously to get the answer because the process is the same. That is, $5.00 a week for 8 weeks is the same as 5 squares in 8 rows, or 40. Now ask your child: "How much money will you have after 9 weeks?" Since $8 \times 5 = 40$, you can show your child that 9×5 *must* equal 45 because we've just increased the number 8 by 1, making it 9, so we just add another 5 squares to the 40 to get 45. So after 9 weeks your child will have $45.00 saved.

Turning the Tables

Now that your child understands what multiplication *looks* like and why it is a special type of addition, it is time to see a multiplication table and *memorize* the multiplication problems and solutions. There is really no way around this process, other than making it easier by first explaining multiplication visually, which we've just done. So turn now to the multiplication tables on the next page, and work on them with your child until they are relatively familiar.

Be sure to show your child how the multiplication table is similar to the multiplication squares on the previous pages, but tell her that symbols are used here in place of the squares. There is a consistency in the structure that allows us to understand why multiplication works the way it does. For example, in the squares game any number multiplied by 0 is 0 and any number multiplied by 1 remains the same. So it is in the multiplication table.

Have your child turn to the multiplication table on the following page and point out to her the sequence of top numbers that runs from 0 to 10, and the sequence of side numbers that also runs from 0 to 10. So the multiplication table is going to multiply all numbers between 0 and 10 with one another. And right away, point out to your child that she already knows many of the answers from what we've done so far. For example, all answers in the top row and in the left column must be 0 because any number multiplied by 0 is 0. Furthermore, all answers in the second row and second column must be the same as the multiplier because anything multiplied by 1 remains the same. In addition, all answers in the third row and third column are just a doubling of the multiplier. Another trick is with the 10's. Tell your child that to multiply any number by 10 you just attach 0 to the end of the number. So 10×5 is just a 5 with a 0 attached, or 50; and 10×10 is a 10 with another 0 on the end, or 100.

Multiplying Fun

There is no getting around the need for your child to practice what she has just learned about multiplication. You can help her by making it as much of a game as possible. One of the standard things to do is to write down the multiplication problems on flash cards (you can use 3" by 5" or 5" by 7" index cards purchased at a stationery store) with the problem written on one side and the answer on the other. "Flash" your child the problem, wait for the answer, then flip the card around to check the verbal answer with the one written on the card.

To make it more fun, you might reward your child for a certain amount of right answers. If when you first start the game she gets 5 out of 10 correct, you could reward her with some candy, or a cookie, or something your child really enjoys. But as she improves, you should up the standard, perhaps rewarding her if she gets 7 out of 10 right, then 9 out of 10, then, finally, 10 out of 10, at which point she will have mastered the multiplication table.

	0	1	2	3	4	5	6	7	8	9	10
0	0 ×0 = 0	1 ×0 = 0	2 ×0 = 0	3 ×0 = 0	4 ×0 = 0	5 ×0 = 0	6 ×0 = 0	7 ×0 = 0	8 ×0 = 0	9 ×0 = 0	10 ×0 = 0
1	0 ×1 = 0	1 ×1 = 1	2 ×1 = 2	3 ×1 = 3	4 ×1 = 4	5 ×1 = 5	6 ×1 = 6	7 ×1 = 7	8 ×1 = 8	9 ×1 = 9	10 ×1 = 10
2	0 ×2 = 0	1 ×2 = 2	2 ×2 = 4	3 ×2 = 6	4 ×2 = 8	5 ×2 = 10	6 ×2 = 12	7 ×2 = 14	8 ×2 = 16	9 ×2 = 18	10 ×2 = 20
3	0 ×3 = 0	1 ×3 = 3	2 ×3 = 6	3 ×3 = 9	4 ×3 = 12	5 ×3 = 15	6 ×3 = 18	7 ×3 = 21	8 ×3 = 24	9 ×3 = 27	10 ×3 = 30
4	0 ×4 = 0	1 ×4 = 4	2 ×4 = 8	3 ×4 = 12	4 ×4 = 16	5 ×4 = 20	6 ×4 = 24	7 ×4 = 28	8 ×4 = 32	9 ×4 = 36	10 ×4 = 40
5	0 ×5 = 0	1 ×5 = 5	2 ×5 = 10	3 ×5 = 15	4 ×5 = 20	5 ×5 = 25	6 ×5 = 30	7 ×5 = 35	8 ×5 = 40	9 ×5 = 45	10 ×5 = 50
6	0 ×6 = 0	1 ×6 = 6	2 ×6 = 12	3 ×6 = 18	4 ×6 = 24	5 ×6 = 30	6 ×6 = 36	7 ×6 = 42	8 ×6 = 48	9 ×6 = 54	10 ×6 = 60
7	0 ×7 = 0	1 ×7 = 7	2 ×7 = 14	3 ×7 = 21	4 ×7 = 28	5 ×7 = 35	6 ×7 = 42	7 ×7 = 49	8 ×7 = 56	9 ×7 = 63	10 ×7 = 70
8	0 ×8 = 0	1 ×8 = 8	2 ×8 = 16	3 ×8 = 24	4 ×8 = 32	5 ×8 = 40	6 ×8 = 48	7 ×8 = 56	8 ×8 = 64	9 ×8 = 72	10 ×8 = 80
9	0 ×9 = 0	1 ×9 = 9	2 ×9 = 18	3 ×9 = 27	4 ×9 = 36	5 ×9 = 45	6 ×9 = 54	7 ×9 = 63	8 ×9 = 72	9 ×9 = 81	10 ×9 = 90
10	0 ×10 = 0	1 ×10 = 10	2 ×10 = 20	3 ×10 = 30	4 ×10 = 40	5 ×10 = 50	6 ×10 = 60	7 ×10 = 70	8 ×10 = 80	9 ×10 = 90	10 ×10 = 100

The Answer Game

You might also try modifying a board game you already play, one that has squares and moving pieces, like Monopoly. Instead of using dice to find the number of squares to move, flash the multiplication card to your child. If she gets the correct answer, she gets to move her game piece the number of squares of the larger multiplier in the flash card problem while you move your piece the number of squares of the smaller multiplier. If she gets the answer wrong, then you move your piece the larger number while she moves her piece the smaller number. This way, if she is getting more right than wrong, she will win the game. Then you might have a prize for the winner, something you would both enjoy winning.

If you don't have a board game, you can use a photocopy of the number box you used earlier. You and your child, each with a different colored pen, pencil, or crayon, can mark squares, depending on your child's correct or incorrect answers. The one with the most squares at the end of the game (after going through many multiplication problems) is the winner.

The Back and Forth Game

One final game you might try with the multiplication table is to take steps forward across the room for each right answer and backward for each wrong answer. If your child gets the right answer he gets to take as many steps as the largest multiplier in the problem; if he gets it wrong, he has to take the same number of steps backward. He "wins" when he gets to the other side of the room by correctly answering enough questions.

Human memory being what it is, we also suggest tackling the multiplication table in bits, doing, perhaps, just a row at a time. Also, your child will need repetition to learn the table completely, so you can use all of these game ideas over the course of several days or weeks until the table is mastered.

Once the multiplication table is mastered you can turn to the multiplication problems—that is, all the 1-digit number multiplication problems that can be found in the multiplication table. As your child works through these, have him double-check his answers with those in the table, as this will reinforce what he has already learned, or teach him new multiplication math skills. If your child is having trouble, remind him of the game of filling in the boxes. For example, for the first row of problems below, you can tell your child: "4 × 4 is the same as 4 rows of desks with 4 desks in each row; how many desks are there in total?" Or: "6 × 3 is the same problem as figuring out your allowance: If you make 6 dollars a week for 3 weeks, how many dollars will you have?" Making the problems practical and useful will make your child more interested in working them out. The answers are at the end of the chapter.

(1)	(2)	(3)	(4)	(5)	(6)
4	6	8	2	7	9
× 4	× 3	× 4	× 3	× 2	× 9

(7)	(8)	(9)	(10)	(11)	(12)
5	1	7	3	4	8
× 7	× 1	× 0	× 3	× 1	× 2

(13)	(14)	(15)	(16)	(17)	(18)
2	3	8	7	7	9
× 0	× 9	× 7	× 7	× 4	× 7

Multiplication with Pigs, Pens, and Pundreds

At this point we want to move on to larger problems, such as the multiplication of 2- and 3-digit numbers. To ease your child into these problems, it might be a good idea to get out the old familiar "Pigs, Pens, and Pundreds" game. We'll start with a problem your child already knows from the multiplication tables:

$$\begin{array}{r} 10 \\ \times\, 5 \\ \hline \end{array}$$

Your child already knows that 10 × 5 = 50, because of the rule you taught him that any number multiplied by 10 is itself with a 0 after it. Another way to state this problem using the "Pigs, Pens, and Pundreds" game is to ask your child: "How many pigs is 5 pens of pigs?"

Well, your child already knows from playing the earlier games that there are 10 pigs in a pen, and 5 pens makes 50 pigs. So multiplying 10 pigs by 5 is the same as having 5 pens.

Let's try a slightly harder one:

$$\begin{array}{r} 14 \\ \times\, 7 \\ \hline \end{array}$$

First of all, remind your child that 14 pigs is 1 pen and 4 loose pigs. Then tell him that the multiplication problem is really how many pigs there will be in total if we lay out on the table 14 pigs, 7 times. Using the loose pigs and pens, your child can first multiply 7 times the 4 loose pigs, which he now knows to be 28. But as he also knows, 28 pigs is 2 pens and 8 pigs. So have him set these aside on the table. Now he multiplies 7 times the 1 pen, which he knows to be 7 pens. Have him group these into a different pile. To get the answer, all he has to do now is add the 7 pens to the 2 pens and 8 pigs, which should be easy, giving 9 pens and 8 pigs, or 98.

See how easy multiplication is when we ease into it slowly? Let's try another one, a little harder but using the same principles.

$$\begin{array}{r} 89 \\ \times\, 6 \\ \hline \end{array}$$

Remind your child that he wants to know what 8 pens and 9 pigs is, 6 times, so he will begin by multiplying the 9 loose pigs by 6, giving 54 pigs, or 5 pens and 4 pigs. Then he will multiply 8 pens by 6, giving 48 pens. Now, with the two groups of 5 pens and 4 pigs and 48 pens, he merely has to add them together, giving a total of 53 pens and 4 pigs. But there is one thing left to do. Since your child also already knows that 10 pens makes a pundred, 53 pens is actually 5 pundreds and 3 pens. So the final answer, through simple conversion and addition, is 5 pundreds, 3 pens, and 4 pigs, or 534. So:

$$89 \times 6 = 534$$

It would probably be a good idea at this point to teach your child the process of doing this same multiplication on paper with numbers instead of using the pigs, pens, and pundreds. These are meant to be a teaching tool, not a replacement for working with numbers, and since some multiplication problems involve really big numbers—more than you've got available in the form of pigs, pens, and pundreds, now is the time to make this transition. Besides, when your child learns this in school, this is how he will be taught.

Say to your child: "Let's try the same multiplication game we just played—this time multiplying 89 times 6, which isn't in the multiplication table. If we break it down into two smaller multiplication games, as we did with the pigs and pens, you'll know how to do it. But now let's do the multiplication problem on paper with numbers instead of using the pigs and pens on the table. Watch: 6 times 9 is what? That's right, 54, so we'll *put down* the 4, which is like the 4 loose pigs, and *carry over* the 5 to the pens side. Now, what's 6 times 8? Right, it's 48. Then we have to add the 5 to the 48, which is 53. So we *bring down* the 53 and we have 534. So 89 times 6 is 534.

$6 \times 9 = 54$

Put down the 4.

Carry the 5.

$6 \times 8 = 48$

$48 + 5 = 53$

Put down the 53.

The answer is 534.

$$\begin{array}{r} 5 \\ 89 \\ \times\, 6 \\ \hline 534 \end{array}$$

Explain to your child that when you "put down the 4 and carry the 5," you're just putting down 4 loose pigs, and carrying 5 pens. So beginning with our pigs-in-a-pen-in-a-pundred game from before, it is easy to see how this works.

We've provided your child with some more problems, below, to work on with numbers on paper instead of with pigs and pens. If you feel it is necessary to return to that teaching tool, then do so, but be sure to work back up to using just numbers. The answers are at the end of the chapter.

(19)	(20)	(21)	(22)	(23)	(24)
11	21	18	12	37	42
× 6	× 6	× 2	× 9	× 3	× 5
66					

(25)	(26)	(27)	(28)	(29)	(30)
19	25	36	99	87	67
× 1	× 5	× 4	× 2	× 2	× 8

(31)	(32)	(33)	(34)	(35)	(36)
13	72	51	92	42	23
× 8	× 3	× 1	× 0	× 6	× 3

(37)	(38)	(39)	(40)	(41)	(42)
39	82	59	62	13	14
× 2	× 5	× 0	× 9	× 3	× 8

(43)	(44)	(45)	(46)	(47)
123	302	200	421	999
× 8	× 3	× 5	× 4	× 1
984				

(48)	(49)	(50)	(51)	(52)
582	113	621	501	801
× 6	× 2	× 8	× 3	× 0

Okay, now we'll try multiplying a 2-digit number by another 2-digit number. The principles we've used before still apply, so let's return to the 10's trick. You taught your child that anything multiplied by 10 is the number with a 0 on the end. We saw that this was the case with 1-digit numbers in the multiplication table, and now you should show your child that this trick applies to *all* numbers. For example, 53 × 10 is 530, or a 53 with a 0 on the end. And 128 × 10 = 1280. Do some of these with your child for practice:

$$62 \times 10 = ?$$
$$168 \times 10 = ?$$
$$396 \times 10 = ?$$
$$2746 \times 10 = ?$$

There is another magic number trick similar to the 10's trick. You can multiply any number by the multiples of 10—20, 30, 40, 50, 60, 70, 80, or 90—and the answer is just the top number multiplied by the number in the tens column below, with a 0 tacked on the end. So 26 × 20 would be 26 × 2, which is 52, with a 0 on the end, or 520. Or 73 × 40 is 73 × 4, or 292 with a 0 on the end, or 2920. And so on. Just as easy is the trick of any number multiplied by 100. It is just the number with two 0's on the end. So 84 × 100 is 8400. And 49 × 100 is 4900.

Armed with this powerful tool, your child can solve the following problem with ease:

$$\begin{array}{r} 13 \\ \times 12 \\ \hline \end{array}$$

First, we can think of 13 × 12 as 13 × 2 plus 13 × 10. Since your child can easily figure 13 × 2 as 26; and since your child knows that 13 × 10 is 13 with a 0 on the end, or 130, he merely has to add 26 to 130 to get the answer of 156. If he doesn't know that 13 × 2 is 26, he can break this smaller problem down further to a simpler multiplication problem (as we did above) of 10 × 2 plus 3 × 2, or 20 + 6 = 26. Then add this to 130 for a total of 156.

One way to think of this trick of breaking down a large multiplication problem into smaller multiplication problems is to have your child imagine that a bank has 13 bags of coins, each bag of which contains 12 coins. In every bag of 12 coins, 10 coins are gold and 2 coins are silver. Now, ask your child: "How many gold coins are there in all the bags? How many silver coins are there?" How many coins are there in all? By the rules of multiplication we can say that the bank has 13 bags of 12 coins each, or 13 × 12, as in the multiplication problem above. But there's another way to get the answer. The bank has 13 times 2 silver coins and 13 times 10 gold coins. So:

Number of silver coins = 13 × 2 =   **26**
Number of gold coins   = 13 × 10 =   **+130**
Total number of coins   =   **156**

Therefore we can see that 13 × 12 can be done two ways: as a straight 13 × 12 = 156, and as 13 × 2 plus 13 × 10 = 156.

Let's do a slightly more complicated problem, but one that your child can once again break down to smaller multiplication problems. Let's try:

$$\begin{array}{r} 42 \\ \times\,16 \\ \hline \end{array}$$

Using the coins game, you might state to your child that we have 42 bags with 16 coins in each bag; 10 coins in each bag are gold and 6 are silver. Then ask your child: "How many gold coins are there? How many silver coins are there?" How many coins are there in all? We can illustrate this problem as follows:

Number of silver coins = 42 × 6 =   **252**
Number of gold coins   = 42 × 10 = **+420**
Total number of coins   =   **672**

In this case your child has already been working problems like 42 × 6, and he just learned, above, that 42 × 10 is simple, because he only has to add a 0 to the end of 42.

Let's try one more, a little harder still:

$$\begin{array}{r} 63 \\ \times\,28 \\ \hline \end{array}$$

In this problem your child can break this down into the coins game as follows:

Number of silver coins = 63 × 8   504
Number of gold coins   = 63 × 20   + 1260
Total number of coins   =   1764

Your child can already work a problem like 63 × 8, and 63 × 20 is just 63 × 2 with a 0 tacked on the end.

Below is a set of multiplication problems for you and your child to practice with, using either the traditional method or, conceptually easier, using the coins game. The answers are at the end of the chapter.

(53)	(54)	(55)	(56)	(57)	(58)
11	18	12	23	19	30
× 10	× 12	× 11	× 18	× 13	× 10

(59)	(60)	(61)	(62)	(63)	(64)
27	40	99	81	47	50
× 20	× 11	× 13	× 30	× 40	× 21

(65)	(66)	(67)	(68)	(69)	(70)
10	33	19	46	52	61
× 10	× 21	× 18	× 13	× 15	× 47

(71) 82 × 25	(72) 35 × 35	(73) 15 × 10	(74) 18 × 14	(75) 31 × 18	(76) 69 × 19
(77) 14 × 14	(78) 62 × 11	(79) 73 × 41	(80) 20 × 12	(81) 19 × 13	(82) 86 × 10
(83) 50 × 25	(84) 25 × 25	(85) 39 × 17	(86) 69 × 59	(87) 47 × 21	(88) 84 × 36

Let's do a larger problem:

$$219 \\ \times 23$$

Start by showing your child the traditional way of solving this problem, then work her through the same problem conceptually with coins. The traditional solving of this multiplication problem looks like this:

$$
\begin{array}{r}
219 \\
\times\,23 \\
\hline
657 \\
+\,4380 \\
\hline
5037
\end{array}
$$

We can interpret this problem by saying we have 219 bags of coins, 23 coins in each bag, 20 of which are gold and 3 of which are silver. Now we multiply:

Number of silver coins = 219 × 3   657
Number of gold coins   = 219 × 20   +4380
Total number of coins =   5037

Finally, we'll multiply a 3-digit number times another 3-digit number:

$$326$$
$$\times\,248$$

In this problem we have 326 bags, with 248 coins in each bag. As we've got a 3-digit number representing the numbers of coins in each bag, we'll need another type of coin. So let's say we've got 326 bags with 248 coins in each, consisting of 200 platinum coins, 40 gold coins, and 8 silver coins.

Proceeding in the usual manner:

Number of silver coins   = 326 × 8
Number of gold coins   = 326 × 40
Number of platinum coins = 326 × 200

This problem really isn't that hard. Your child can already do 326 × 8, and 326 × 40 is just 326 × 4 with a 0 tacked on the end. Likewise, 326 × 200 is just 326 × 2 with two 0's on the end. Thus:

$$326$$
$$\times\,248$$

326 × 8 =	2608
326 × 40 =	13040
326 × 200 =	+65200
Total =	80848

On the following pages we've provided a series of 3-digit numbers to be multiplied by 2-digit numbers and 3-digit numbers. The answers follow. At this point your child has really mastered multiplication at a very advanced level, so be sure to congratulate your child on doing such a great job. You can, of course, return to this chapter for practice whenever it is needed.

Now, let's go to the next and final chapter—on division! At this point, we feel your child is prepared to play yet another fun game of math.

(89)	(90)	(91)
201	136	333
× 13	× 21	× 11

(92)	(93)	(94)
157	259	500
× 36	× 10	× 20

(95)	(96)	(97)
901	628	732
× 59	× 37	× 43

(98)	(99)	(100)
222	409	659
× 111	× 100	× 201

(101)	(102)	(103)
900	762	529
× 201	× 137	× 342

(104)	(105)	(106)
637	525	999
× 119	× 125	× 111

CHAPTER

8

Divide and Conquer: Division Games

The next time you and your child want to share some cookies, you can teach him about division by having him *share*, or *divide*, the total number of cookies evenly between the two of you. Let's say you've got a small bag with 6 cookies in it. You instruct your child to divide the cookies evenly. Perhaps he empties the bag on the table and says, "One for you, one for me, another for you, and another for me, and a third one for you and a third one for me."

So 6 cookies shared by 2 people leaves 3 cookies for each. Your child has just done a division problem that we would write out as $6 \div 2 = 3$, or, in words, six divided by two equals three. Have your child play more of these sorts of basic division games, taking, say, 8 candies and sharing them evenly between 2 people. Or get a pile of 12 pennies and share them equally between 2 people, 6 for each. You might try having your child divide his toys into piles, taking out, say, 10 toys and dividing them into 2 equal piles, 5 toys in each pile. Here are some practice sharing problems for your child, dividing by 2:

$2 \div 2$
$16 \div 2$
$6 \div 2$

10 ÷ 2
20 ÷ 2
8 ÷ 2
12 ÷ 2
4 ÷ 2
14 ÷ 2
18 ÷ 2

But as you and your child may have noticed, all of these division problems result in an equal number for both people. What happens when we divide a number by 2 and there is something "left over"? For example, what if you have 7 cookies to share between you and your child? She will quickly see that you each get 3 cookies, but there is 1 cookie left over, or remaining. In division problems this "left over" number is called the "remainder." So when we divide 7 by 2 we say that the answer is 3 with a remainder of 1. Here are some practice problems for your child which have remainders:

9 ÷ 2
13 ÷ 2
11 ÷ 2
17 ÷ 2
3 ÷ 2
15 ÷ 2
5 ÷ 2
19 ÷ 2
7 ÷ 2

We don't always divide things by 2, of course, so you might want to have your child do some division problems with numbers greater than 2. For example, perhaps you could have your child divide the cookies into 3 piles, in which case she would take the total of 6 cookies and put 2 into each pile so that 6 ÷ 3 = 2. Or have your child divide 15 pennies into 5 piles so that there are 3 pennies in each, or 15 ÷ 5 = 3.

Or let's try a slightly harder one. Have your child divide 17 pennies by 3. As she will see, this does not divide equally, as it gives 5 pennies with a remainder of 2.

In these problems your child will not automatically know what a number can be divided into. For example, she won't know that the 12 cookies she has can be divided by 3 (to share with her two friends) without placing the cookies into piles, one at a time. Shortly, however, we will see how to do this faster. Here are some practice division problems with numbers greater than 2, some of which divide evenly and some of which leave a remainder:

12 ÷ 3

7 ÷ 4

15 ÷ 3

11 ÷ 5

14 ÷ 5

9 ÷ 1

20 ÷ 3

8 ÷ 6

13 ÷ 5

10 ÷ 4

Dividing with Pigs and Pens

Now suppose we wanted to do a larger problem, like 84 ÷ 4. Since it would be difficult to find 84 loose objects around the house, and even more tedious to divide them into 4 groups, let's return to our standard teaching tool: the "Pigs, Pens, and Pundreds" game. Here is an excellent way to show your child how a number can be evenly divided or unevenly divided, leaving numbers or, in this case, pigs, "left over." Try working:

36 ÷ 3

First have your child arrange 36 pigs on the table, which she should do as 3 pens and 6 pigs. After dividing them into 3 equal groups (that is, each with the same number of pens and pigs) she will see that each group contains 1 pen and 2 loose pigs. Since your child knows that 1 pen and 2 pigs is 12, the answer to 36 ÷ 3 is 12. Let's try some practice division problems using pens and pigs that can be evenly divided:

84 ÷ 4
82 ÷ 2
77 ÷ 7
93 ÷ 3
80 ÷ 4
55 ÷ 5
60 ÷ 6

We'll now do another division problem of similar size, but one that will require your child to trade in pens for loose pigs:

$$24 \div 6$$

If your child lays out 24 pigs on the table in the usual manner of 2 pens and 4 pigs, he will soon see that there are not enough pens to go around, so he will have to trade in the pens for pigs, giving a total of 24 loose pigs (20 from the pens, plus 4 loose ones). Then he can begin to divide the 24 into 6 different piles. After your child has dispersed the 24 pigs into 6 different piles, there will be 4 pigs in each pile. Ask your child how many pigs there are altogether. Probably he will remember the total is 24 pigs. Another way of saying this is: How many *times* does 6 go into 24? The answer is 4 *times*. So we can reverse the division problem and say that 6 *times* 4 equals 24.

$$6 \times 4 = 24$$
$$24 \div 6 = 4$$

One way of checking your division answer is to reverse the problem—that is, by multiplying—and verify that:

$$4 \times 6 = 24$$

Next, let's look at a problem that has a remainder and see how we can check the answer through multiplication. We'll try:

17 ÷ 3

After sorting the pigs into the 3 piles your child will have 5 pigs in each pile, with a remainder of 2. To check this, he can multiply 5 × 3, getting 15, and then add the 2 left over to give us our original 17 pigs. That is,

$$5 \times 3 + 2 = 17$$

Here are some more practice division problems that divide evenly for you to work on with your child. For some of them, your child will have to trade in pens for loose pigs.

20 ÷ 4

24 ÷ 3

32 ÷ 8

54 ÷ 6

49 ÷ 7

36 ÷ 4

81 ÷ 9

35 ÷ 7

36 ÷ 9

64 ÷ 8

Let's try another, larger division problem, one that not only requires trading in pens but also leaves a remainder because it can't be divided evenly:

82 ÷ 3

First have your child arrange 82 pigs on the table, which he will do as 8 pens and 2 pigs. He will then try to divide them into 3 equal groups. He will soon see that this division process doesn't come out as an even number of pens and pigs. He will have 3 groups with 2 pens in each group, but with 2 pens and 2 pigs remaining. He'll now have to change the 2 pens into 20 loose pigs which, added to the 2 he already has, makes 22 pigs.

Next he must distribute the 22 loose pigs into the 3 groups. Perhaps he will begin by moving 5 loose pigs into each of the 3 piles of pens and pigs, and that's fine but he'll still have 7 loose pigs left over. These can be divided still further, of course, so your child will move 2 loose pigs into each of the 3 groups, finally ending up with only 1 loose pig left over.

Then he merely has to count up or add the number of pens and pigs in each group, which is 27. So the answer to the problem of 82 ÷ 3 is 27 with 1 left over.

Below we present a visual demonstration of what this problem might look like with pens and pigs on your table arranged into 3 groups:

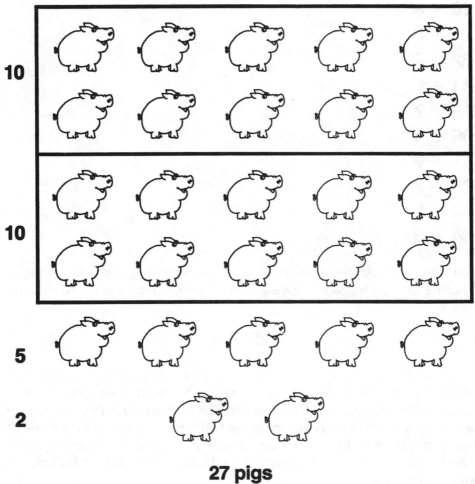

27 pigs

10

10

5

2

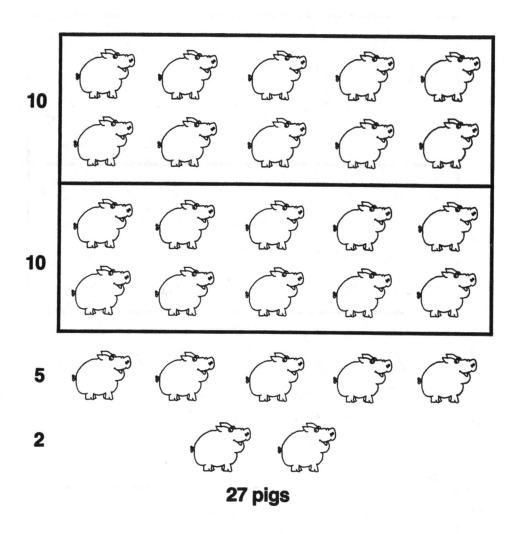

27 pigs

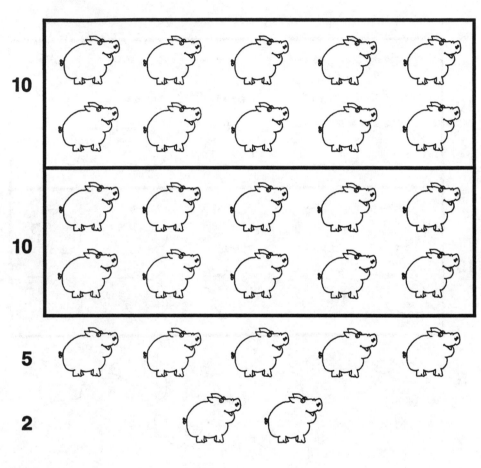

10

10

5

2

27 pigs

**with 1
left over**

Arranging this many pens and pigs can sometimes be cumbersome, especially when we are working with 3-digit numbers, so we want to show your child another way to work this out in a process called "long division." In this process, another way to write down 82 ÷ 3 is:

$$3\overline{)82}$$

or, as we would say, "three divided into eighty-two."

When the division problem is done in *long division*, it helps to know the names of the various numbers involved. In this case, the special names are as follows:

27 r 1   *Quotient (remainder)*
Divisor → 3)82 *← Dividend*

The number you divide into is called the "dividend." In this problem, 82 is the dividend.

The number you divide by is called the "divisor." In this problem, 7 is the divisor.

The answer is called the "quotient." In this problem, 27 r 1 is the quotient ("r 1" means remainder 1). We can write this problem out like this:

82   ÷   3   =   27 r 1
Dividend ÷ Divisor = Quotient (remainder)

So, when we divide 3 into 82, the question is, how can we share, or distribute, 82 into 3 different groups? We saw how to do this with pens and pigs. Now let's see how it's done in long division:

$$\begin{array}{r} 27 \text{ r } 1 \\ 3\overline{)82} \\ 6 \\ \hline 22 \\ 21 \\ \hline 1 \end{array}$$

Just as in the pens and pigs example of this problem, we began distributing pens first. We asked ourselves, "How many ways can we share, or distribute, 8 pens into 3 groups?" or "How many times does 3 go into 8?" We also learned that we can check division answers with multiplication. Let's try that here: What number times 3 equals 8?

At this point you and your child may have to use the trial-and-error method. Since 3 doesn't go into 8 evenly, we may first try 1 × 3, but that is too low. Then we may try 3 × 3, but that is too high. Finally, we try 2 × 3, and that gives us 6, which is pretty close, so we put down the 6 below the 8. Then we subtract and write down what's left over when we take 6 from 8, which is 2. We write the 2 down below the 6.

Now we've got 2 pens left over. Next, we bring down the 2 leftover pigs and put them next to the 2 pens, making 22 loose pigs. Now we divide these 22 pigs by 3. We ask, "How many times does 3 go into 22?" Again, by trial and error, you and your child can try multiplying numbers. What number times 3 equals 22? Since 3 doesn't go into 22 evenly, you can try different numbers—3 × 6 is 18, but 3 × 7 is 21, which is even closer (3 × 8 is 24, which is too large). So we use 7, putting it next to the 2 in the quotient, and putting down the 21 under the 22. Now we subtract and find we have 1 pig left over, so we bring him down under the 1, and that becomes our remainder, which we put in the quotient after 27.

So in long division, as with pens and pigs, 82 ÷ 3 = 27 r 1. We can check this by observing that 3 × 27 + 1 = 82.

The following 10 practice division problems leave remainders and, as before, some of them will require that your child trade in pens for pigs. After working them out with pens and pigs, we suggest you have your child do them in long division as he just learned above. Also have your child verify the answers by multiplying, and then adding in the remainders.

24 ÷ 5

40 ÷ 7

65 ÷ 4

38 ÷ 3

72 ÷ 7

58 ÷ 6

98 ÷ 9

27 ÷ 8

53 ÷ 2

35 ÷ 6

Next, we'll show you how to teach your child to do 3-digit division problems, beginning with a simple one that can be divided evenly:

$$693 \div 3$$

or

$$3\overline{)693}$$

For this problem your child will need all the pundreds, pens, and pigs he has used in the past. Laying out 6 pundreds, 9 pens, and 3 pigs, the division problem requires your child to divide them into 3 equal piles. He can do this problem either from right to left, or left to right. In the former, he takes the 6 pundreds and divides them into 3 piles, with 2 pundreds in each pile. Then he takes the 9 pens and places them into the 3 piles, putting 3 pens in each. Finally, he puts the 3 pigs into the 3 piles, 1 pig in each. Thus, in each pile your child has put 2 pundreds, 3 pens, and 1 pig, or 231. So:

693 ÷ 3 = 231

or, in long division:

```
      231
  3)693
    6
    ──
    09
     9
    ──
    03
     3
    ──
     0
```

Now we'll try another 3-digit number that can be divided evenly, but this time the problem is slightly harder:

$$408 \div 4$$
$$\text{or}$$
$$4\overline{)408}$$

As usual, begin by having your child lay out 408 pigs on the table (not 408 loose pigs, of course, but 4 pundreds, 0 pens, and 8 pigs). She merely has to separate them into 4 equal piles, placing 1 pundred in each pile and 2 pigs in each pile. Thus, each of the 4 piles has 1 pundred and 2 pigs in it, or 102. So:

$$408 \div 4 = 102$$

You can have your child work this out in long division, following the same process she just learned. We illustrate this one for you to show your child.

$$
\begin{array}{r}
102 \\
4\overline{)408} \\
\underline{4} \\
00 \\
\underline{0} \\
08 \\
\underline{8} \\
0
\end{array}
$$

This one is very simple, as 4 can be shared by 4 groups just once, or 4 goes into 4 just 1 time, with 0 pundreds left over. Since there are no pens, we can say that 4 goes into 0, 0 times (remember from multiplication that any number times 0 is always 0), so we put down the 0 in the quotient and in the computation, and then ask, "How many times does 4 go into 8?" Since your child knows that $2 \times 4 = 8$, she knows that 4 goes into 8 twice. So we write down the 2 in a quotient. She can check her answer by multiplying 2×4 and putting down the answer of 8 at the bottom of the computation and by subtracting 8 from 8, which will give her 0. Then she'll know there are no pigs left over. So, as before, $408 \div 4 = 102$.

We will now try one along these same lines, though again slightly harder:

$$588 \div 7$$
or
$$7\overline{)588}$$

When your child lays out the number 588 as 5 pundreds, 8 pens, and 8 pigs and attempts to divide the 5 pundreds into 7 equal piles, he will immediately see that this cannot be done as 2 of the piles would have no pundreds in them. The 5 pundreds must be traded in for 50 pens, giving a total of 58 pens when the other 8 are included. Then he can begin to place the pens into 7 piles. Since he doesn't know how many pens will fit into each pile, he will have to experiment with different numbers, maybe putting in 3 pens at a time or 5 pens at a time. But eventually he will end up with 8 pens in each pile, with 2 pens left over. And, as we saw previously, the 2 pens can be traded in for 20 loose pigs, for a total of 28 loose pigs to be divided into the 7 piles. Through trial and error your child will eventually come to put 4 pigs into each of the 7 piles, leaving a total of 8 pens and 4 pigs in each pile. So:

$$588 \div 7 = 84$$
or, in long division:

```
    84
7)588
   56↓
   028
    28
     0
```

We can verify that this is correct by multiplying 7 × 84, which gives us 588.

Now let's try a 3-digit problem that does not divide evenly. Your child's answer will have a remainder:

$$967 \div 2$$
or
$$2\overline{)967}$$

First your child will lay out the number 967 with pundreds, pens, and pigs—9 pundreds, 6 pens, and 7 pigs. This problem is interesting because when your child divides the 9 pundreds into 2 piles she will be left with 4 pundreds in each pile, and 1 pundred left over to be divided between the two. This requires that your child break up the pundred into 10 pens. Since the number 967 already has 6 pens in it— that is, there are already 6 pens there on the table, she can combine them for a total of 16 pens, and then divide them up into the 2 piles, putting 8 pens in each pile. That leaves 7 pigs to be separated, which she can do by putting 3 pigs in each pile, leaving a *remainder* of 1 pig.

So in each of the 2 piles there are 4 pundreds, 8 pens, and 3 pigs, or 483, with a remainder of 1, which we can designate with a small "r." So:

$$967 \div 2 = 483 \, r \, 1$$

You can also have your child work out the problem in long division on a sheet of paper, and then check his computations with our illustration of the problem, below:

```
      483 r 1
   2)967
      8↓
      16
      16↓
      07
       6
       1
```

Verify by multiplying 2 × 483 and adding 1, to get 967.

Once your child has mastered long division, it becomes easy to divide a 1-digit number into practically *any* number, no matter how long it is. For example, let's try a division problem with a 5-digit dividend:

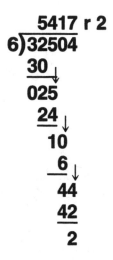

So even though dividing 6 into a huge number like 32504 sounds intimidating, it really isn't once your child grasps the concept of distributing pundreds, pens, and pigs, and masters the skill of doing long division, both of which your child should be getting good at by now.

Just to reinforce all these great math talents your child now has, we've provided some more long division problems, increasing in difficulty. Your child will probably find long division faster than using the pundreds, pens, and pigs. The answers follow.

①

2)867

②

3)201

③

4)101

④

5)506

⑤
6)298

⑥
7)341

⑦
8)782

⑧
9)672

⑨
5)4728

⑩
7)3967

⑪
3)84629

⑫
6)38562

⑬
9)204804

⑭
5)703972

⑮
7)360711

⑯
2)509178

Answers

1.	**433 r 1**	**2.**	**67**	**3.**	**25 r 1**	**4.**	**101 r 1**
5.	**49 r 4**	**6.**	**48 r 5**	**7.**	**97 r 6**	**8.**	**74 r 6**
9.	**945 r 3**	**10.**	**566 r 5**	**11.**	**28209 r 2**	**12.**	**6427**
13.	**22756**	**14.**	**140794 r 2**	**15.**	**51530 r 1**	**16.**	**254589**

CHAPTER

9

Problem Solving: Taking Basic Skills to the Next Level

Critical thinking is, without a doubt, the most crucial aspect of math. Basically, critical thinking involves using basic mathematical skills as they apply to the real world. It is probably the most gratifying aspect of math since it allows the *user* to see how math skills are put to use. It is very important to stress the importance of problem solving since higher levels of math require greater skills, not to mention the fact that advanced levels of math, including algebra and geometry, require strong problem solving abilities.

Problem solving, more often called word problems at the elementary level, usually enter the curriculum by third grade, sometimes sooner. The object is to introduce and familiarize the student with the concept of basic problem solving and the most elementary strategies involved. Most critical is the idea that problem solving makes a child think. This is extremely important, since most children, when learning basic math skills, learn in a very concrete or visual manner. In problem solving, the child will have to analyze a situation before attempting to concretely solve the problem.

A child will be required to read a problem first and then determine which operation they must use to solve it. This may sound very simplistic to most adults, but it can be extremely difficult and oftentimes very trying for a child. At the early levels, children have the greatest difficulty determining whether they should add, subtract, multiply, or divide to reach their answer. They are unsure of how to make that determination. Sometimes a problem may even require more than one operation to solve. Then a child will have to decide which operation(s) to use and in which order he must use them. This can become very frustrating to a child. Don't be surprised if, at first, your child gets confused or frustrated. This is quite normal. Actually, your patience is the most critical element in problem solving. Frequently, a child will guess at an answer, since this will not force him to make the initial determination. Guessing is the quickest, the easiest, and the least painful way of arriving at an answer.

The best way to initiate the process of introducing problem solving is to read a problem with your child and decide together which word(s) will help you arrive at an answer. It is very important that time is spent helping your child identify the *key words* in a problem. *Key words* are those words, in the area of problem solving, that tell you which operation you will use to solve a problem. These key words will ultimately determine how well your child solves problems. It is very important to spend a great deal of time on key words.

I have taken the liberty of listing some of the most common key words found in elementary problem solving. I have also provided the mathematical significance of each word or phrase so you know how they will be used in this area of mathematics.

Key Word or Phrase	Meaning
Altogether	Addition
In all	Addition
More/More than	Addition/Subtraction
Plus	Addition
Sum	Addition
Total	Addition
Difference	Subtraction
Less/Less than	Subtraction
Minus	Subtraction
Take away	Subtraction
Product	Multiplication
Times	Multiplication
Of	Multiplication
Divide/Divided by	Division
Quotient	Division

Please note that "More/More than" can be either addition or subtraction. It depends on how the word(s) are used in the problem. Look at these examples carefully and you'll see what I mean.

Example 1:   William has 8 model airplanes hanging from the ceiling in his room. If he hangs 3 *more,* how many will he then have hanging in his room?

Example 2:   Alex collects marbles. He now has 83 in his collection. His friend Mark has 66 marbles in his collection. How many marbles *more than* Mark does Alex has?

In Example 1, William is *adding* model airplanes to his room, therefore indicating the operation of addition. However, in Example 2, we are *comparing* the number of marbles Alex has to the number of marbles Mark has. The comparison is what tells us to find the difference or subtract. Whenever we are comparing, we will always subtract to solve the problem.

In the previous paragraph, the underlined words represent our *keys* to identifying the operation we must use to solve each problem correctly.

Now, here are several more for you to try. Please remember we are *only* trying to identify the operation to solve each problem. Do not try to solve them. Just identify which of the four basic operations (addition, subtraction, multiplication, or division) you will need to use to solve each problem correctly.

Key Words

Circle the key word(s) in each problem and then check your answer at the end of the chapter:

1.   Tyler collects baseball cards. He has 135 baseball cards as of yesterday. This morning he bought 30 more baseball cards. How many baseball cards does he have now?

2.   Susan has 28 roses in her garden. She wants to cut 10 roses to put in a vase in her house. How many less will she have?

3.   Alan has 15 crayons in his backpack. Alisa has 18 crayons in her backpack. How many do they have altogether?

4.   Jeff has collected $4.25 for the school candy drive. Barbara has collected $6.50. How much more has Barbara collected than Jeff?

5.   Sid works at the local supermarket and earns $11.50 per hour. Adele works in a toy store and earns $8.75 per hour. What is the difference between their wages?

6.   Elliot walks 5 miles each day for exercise. Debbie walks 3 miles each day. How many miles less than Elliot does Debbie walk each day?

7.   Phyllis went to the grocery store to get a few items. She spent $3.75 on coffee, $2.25 on milk, and $1.85 on bread. What is the total cost of these items?

8.   Betty works in an office as a secretary. She types 200 words per minute on her typewriter. This is 2 times as fast as her sister Charlotte can type. How many words can Charlotte type in one-minute?

9.   Lowell takes his 3 sons to a baseball game. He has exactly $20.00 in his wallet. He wants to divide the money evenly. How much money can he spend on each person, including himself?

10. Brett and Kurt are going on a field trip at school. There will be two school buses to take the students to the zoo. Each bus will hold 60 students. How many students will the two buses hold in all?

Now that you understand how to find the *key words,* let's put this into practice. It is very important to *always* identify them first. When you have identified the key words, you will know what to do to solve each problem. We are now going to look at problems that involve the operation of addition. You will first want to review those key words that are used for this operation. It will be very helpful to review the key words regularly to reinforce their importance. It is important to teach your child how to analyze *and* organize the problem before attempting to solve it. A simple discussion about the problem will help your child understand the logic behind solving it. Let me explain.

When we look at a word problem, we must first read the problem *several* times to understand its meaning and also to determine what we are being asked to find. This identification process should help us understand what we are going to do to solve the problem and why. The key words are simply the catalyst.

Read the example problem several times and determine what you are being asked to find. Then identify the key words that lead you to the correct operation. For example: William has a marble collection at home. In this collection are 23 clear marbles, 12 green marbles, 18 blue marbles, and 31 multicolored marbles. Today, he is planning to trade some marbles with his friend Alex. He is giving Alex 3 multicolored marbles for 2 clear marbles and 4 green marbles for 2 blue marbles. After trading with Alex, how many marbles will he have altogether in his collection?

After reading this problem several times, we can see that the word *altogether* means we are going to be adding up the total of marbles in his collection. However, we have other operations to perform before we get to that point. Most importantly, this problem needs to be read several times before an attempt is made to solve it.

We need to determine exactly *what* we are being asked to find. The wording of the problem dramatically determines *how* we solve it. What if the final statement of the problem said, "How many red marbles would William have in his collection after the trade?" We would definitely look at this problem quite differently.

Let's look at how we should solve this problem. Strategically, I would solve this problem by first adding up all the marbles in William's collection:

23 clear + 12 green + 18 blue + 31 multicolored = 84 marbles

Next I would subtract the marbles William is trading to Alex:

84 marbles total − (3 multicolored + 4 green) = 77 marbles

Finally, I would add the marbles he is receiving from Alex in the trade:

77 marbles + (2 clear + 2 blue) = 81 marbles

Therefore, William will have 81 marbles in his collection after the trade with Alex. Be certain that you are taking the time to examine your steps in a problem and that you are reading the information correctly before you begin. Formulate a strategy to solve the problem before you actually begin implementing the various operations to solve.

Now we are going to test your problem solving skills. The word problems that follow are divided into the levels of difficulty. Part A is the easiest level; Part B is a little more difficult; and Part C is the most difficult. I strongly encourage you work through all the sections together. I do not recommend skipping Parts A and B because you think your child is ready for the advanced section. Parts A and B provide a solid preliminary foundation to help your child understand the format, the approach and the elements necessary to become an excellent problem solver. The old adage, "Practice makes perfect" is certainly fitting here.

The next five sections follow the sequence of presentation in the book. First we will explore addition problems followed by subtraction, then multiplication and division. Finally, I have added a section that involves more than one step or one operation to solve. The last section is *only* recommended for those children who have mastered the other four sections. The answers to each of the sections are at the end of the chapter. Good luck and enjoy!

Problem Solving with Addition

Part A

1.   Richard is outside playing with his toys. He has 12 cars and 9 trucks. How many toys is he playing with altogether?

2.   Dale is beginning to collect baseball cards. He has 6 cards at home. He just bought 10 more. How many does he have now?

3.   Betty has 2 pairs of blue shorts, 1 pair of red shorts, and 2 pairs of green shorts. How many pairs of shorts does Betty have?

4.   Gail is brushing her hair for school. She has 1 red ribbon, 1 blue ribbon, 1 green ribbon and 1 black ribbon. How many hair ribbons does she have altogether?

5.   Lee's crayon box has 4 red crayons, 5 blue crayons, and 6 green crayons. How many crayons does Lee have in all?

Part B

6.   Alan is cleaning his tool chest in the garage. In his tool chest he has 4 hammers, 9 wrenches, 8 screwdrivers, and 3 saws. How many tools does Alan have in his tool chest in all?

7.   Lowell has to count the number of televisions he has in his store. He has 24 small televisions and 12 large televisions. How many does he have altogether?

8.   Lisa and Karen are going to the supermarket together. Lisa needs to buy 1 carton of milk, 1 loaf of bread, 1 carton of eggs, and 3 bottles of soda. Karen needs to buy 2 bottles of soda, 1 loaf of bread, 1 package of bologna, and 3 bottles of water. How many items are they buying altogether?

9.   Charlotte is having a party at her home tonight. She is going to buy 24 paper plates, 24 paper cups, and 24 plastic spoons. How many items is she planning to buy in all?

10. Aaron wants to buy several CDs to add to his collection. He already has 14 classical, 23 country and western, and 32 easy listening CDs. If he purchases 1 more of each type that he has, how many CDs will he have in all?

Part C

11. Barbara wants to put new ceramic tile in her kitchen. She has 150 tiles in her garage. She also has 35 tiles in the trunk of her car. She thought this was enough to finish the job. After she measured her kitchen floor, she found out that she needed 50 more tiles. How many tiles will she use in all to tile her kitchen floor?

12. Tom is adding a family room onto his house. The room will measure 25 feet long by 15 feet wide. After he finishes building the room addition, he decides to paint the walls. Each long wall totals 200 square feet and each short wall totals 120 square feet. How many square feet will he paint altogether? (Hint remember there are 2 long walls and 2 short walls in the room.)

13. Brett is an expert skier. One day he decides to find out how many feet he will ski in all. The first ski run is 2,755 feet long, the second run is 3,672 feet long, the third run is 2,844 feet long, and the fourth run is 1,988 feet long. After the fourth run, he decides to eat lunch. How many feet did Brett ski altogether before he ate lunch?

14. Kurt likes to ride his bicycle on Saturdays. One Saturday, he decided to ride to the park to play with his friend, William. The distance from Kurt's home to the park is 14 blocks. When they were finished playing, they decided to go and buy ice cream. The distance from the park to the ice cream store is 9 blocks. After they finished their ice cream they decided to go back to the park to play some more. From there, Kurt went home. How many blocks did Kurt ride his bicycle altogether?

15. The Andersen family is going to a picnic on Sunday sponsored by their childrens' school. Mr. Andersen will bring 2 sandwiches and 2 softdrinks for the picnic. Mrs. Andersen will bring 1 sandwich, 2 softdrinks, and 1 bag of potato chips for the picnic. Their two sons will each bring 1 sandwich and 1 softdrink for the picnic. Mrs. Andersen wants to put all of the items into a cooler for the picnic. How many items will have to fit in the cooler so that everything will stay cold at the picnic?

Problem Solving with Subtraction

Part A

1.   Elliot has 9 silver coins that he has saved. He put them in a drawer so that they would be safe. This evening he went to get them to show a friend. He could only find 6 silver coins. How many were missing?

2.   Debbie uses baking sheets to bake cookies for her family. She has 6 baking sheets in her kitchen cabinet. She used 3 of the baking sheets to bake cookies today. How many baking sheets does she still have in the kitchen cabinet?

3.   Amy is starting college this year. She is renting an apartment that has room enough for 4 people. How many more people can share the apartment with Amy this year?

4.   Rian has 5 dollars in his wallet. He needs to buy a notebook for school that costs 3 dollars. After he buys the notebook, how much money will he have left?

5.   Will is saving money to go on a camping trip with his friends. The trip costs 9 dollars for gasoline for his car. Right now he has 4 dollars in his bank. How much more does he need to pay for the gasoline?

Part B

6.   Linda bought 60 tulip bulbs to plant around her house. She has already planted 37 tulip bulbs. How many tulip bulbs does she have left to plant?

7.   Jeff is making room in his yard to build a new brick BBQ. He has been collecting used bricks to build the BBQ. So far, he has collected 167 used bricks. He needs a total of 335 used bricks for the BBQ. How many more does he need to collect before he can build his BBQ?

8.   Melissa brought a set of color markers to her friend's house. They were working on a school project together. There were 48 different color markers in the set. When she came home, she only had 29 markers in her bookbag. How many markers did Melissa leave at her friend's house?

9.   Andrew wants to buy an old silver dollar from the local coin shop. The coin costs $298. Andrew only has $159 saved so far. How much more does he need to save for the silver dollar?

10.   Douglas is shopping around for a new car. The latest model that he would like to purchase costs $13,950. He has to make a down payment of $2,790. How much more would he owe for the car after the down payment?

Part C

11.   Melissa is shopping around for auto insurance for her new car. She has the two best quotes so far and they are $1,947 for one year from the Jones Agency and $2,033 from the Firestein Agency. Which is the best quote and by how much?

12.   Alex is opening a new hardware store in the center of town. Altogether, it cost him $38,953 to open the store. After the first year, his gross revenue was $34,699. How much more revenue did he need to pay for the total cost of opening the store.

13.   Mark works part-time at a horseback riding stable. One of his jobs is to maintain the feed bin for the horses. The capacity of the feed bin is 1,275 quarts. Right now, 1,199 quarts have been used to feed the horses. How much feed should Mark order to completely fill the bin?

14.   Dale is reading a novel for his advanced literature class in high school. The novel has 1,233 pages. He needs to finish reading the book by tomorrow. So far he has read 1,099 pages. If he can read 125 pages in one day, will he be able to finish on time? If not, how many pages will still be left to read?

15.   William loves to climb rocks when he has the time. The last time he went climbing, he climbed 2,761 feet. His record for climbing in one day is 3,351 feet. How many feet short of his record was he on this day?

Problem Solving with Multiplication

Part A

1.   Elesa is using small jars to keep her buttons in. She has 4 jars. There are 5 buttons in each jar. How many buttons does she have in all?

2. Larry works many hours at his job as a lawyer. He works 6 days each week. He works 9 hours each day. How many hours does Larry work in one week?

3. Stephanie makes $3 per hour babysitting. Her friend, Kim, makes 2 times as much as Stephanie. How much money does Kim get paid each hour?

4. Adele writes to many of her friends each week. Last week, she mailed 9 letters. At this rate, how many will she mail in 4 weeks?

5. Marc puts his pocket change on his dresser each night. Last night, he put 7 dimes on his dresser. How much money, in dimes, did Marc put on his dresser?

Part B

6. Alexandra collects miniature dolls from around the world. She currently has 26 dolls in her collection. She estimates that her dolls are worth about $8 each. At this rate, about how much is Alexandra's miniature doll collection worth?

7. Beth likes to save quarters until she fills a jar. Then she takes them to the bank and exchanges them for cash. Right now, Beth has 36 quarters in her jar. How much money has Beth saved in her quarter jar? (Remember each quarter is worth 25¢.)

8. Megan has to write 4 term papers for her classes by the end of the term. Each of these papers has to be a minimum of 15 pages. How many pages, at least, does Megan have to write for all 4 term papers combined?

9. Sue gets the daily newspaper delivered to her house. It costs her 50¢ per day for this service, including the cost of the newspaper. How much does it cost her for 1 month? (Hint 30 days = 1 month)

10. Laurie teaches math in a local junior high school. There are 37 students in each of her classes. Laurie teaches 5 classes each day. How many students does Laurie teach in all of her classes combined?

Part C

11. Karen loves to travel. Her average flying distance per trip is about 2,200 miles round trip. Over the last five years, Karen's trips have totaled 24 in all. About how many miles has Karen traveled over the last five years?

12. Mike works in construction. During the past year he worked on 43 different jobs. The average amount earned per job during that year was about $1,300. About how much in all did Mike earn over the past year?

13. Lance does a great deal of driving visiting clients on his sales job. He travels at an average speed of 45 miles per hour. Last week, he drove a total of 28 hours on his job. How many miles did he drive in all last week?

14. Marty spends $1.27 per gallon of gas. The gas tank in his car will hold 23 gallons. How much will it cost Marty to fill his tank if it is completely empty?

15. When Paul is on the freeway, he averages 65 miles per hour. If his destination is 11 hours away, how far will Paul travel in 11 hours? (Assume Paul is not making any stops on his way.)

Problem Solving with Division

Part A

1. Jennifer and her two closest friends have a total of 9 stuffed animals. Each of the 3 girls has the same number of stuffed animals. How many stuffed animals does each girl have?

2. Abbie and Sarah ordered a medium pizza to share. There are 8 slices of pizza in 1 medium pizza. How many slices will each girl have if they divide the pizza evenly?

3. Karen bought 12 books at the book fair for her 3 children. She wants to give each child the same number of books. How many books should she give each child?

4. Max has 20 minutes left at the batting cages. He wants to divide the time evenly between his 2 sons. How much time will each son get in the batting cage with their dad?

5. Eric, Matt, and Mike are taking turns on a swing in the park. They only want to stay another 15 minutes. How much time will each boy have on the swing if they divide the time evenly?

Part B

6. Vincent is bringing $3.50 to the baseball game so that he can buy a candy bar for each of his friends. Vincent is expecting 5 friends to meet him at the game. Each candy bar costs 75¢. Is Vincent bringing enough money to buy each friend a candy bar?

7. Jason and Charlie are going to the arcade. On the way they meet Clint and Victor. When they arrive at the arcade, they decide to put all their money together and divide it evenly. Altogether they have $8.92. How much money will each boy have to spend at the arcade?

8. Adrienne and her science class are going on a field trip to the museum. There are 36 students in her class altogether. They will be traveling on 2 buses. How many students will travel on each bus if the group is divided evenly?

9. John and Carlos are going to purchase 20 comic books at the store. The total cost of the comic books is $17.80. All the comic books are the same price. What is the unit cost (the cost of 1) of the comic books?

10. This week, peaches are on sale at the supermarket at the rate of 5 pounds for $3.95. At that rate, what is the cost per pound or unit cost of peaches?

Part C

11. Bruce's scouting group is going camping for the weekend. There are 277 scouts in the entire group. Each campground site can only accommodate 65 scouts. How many sites will Bruce's scouting group need to go camping?

12. The local college graduating class this June will have 2,500 students in it. The auditorium can only hold 700 students and their guests at one time. How many different graduations will have to be held to hold all the graduates?

13. Sue is buying beads for the summer craft class she teaches. She decided to buy 3 bags of red beads for a total of 750 beads. There are 35 students enrolled in her class. She wants to divide the beads as evenly as she can. What is the largest number of beads Sue can give each student?

14. Victor and Carrie are having a birthday party for their son, Alex. They have invited 10 of Alex's friends, but only 9 of them can make it. That means there will be exactly 10 children in attendance. They will be going to the skating rink for this party. The cost per child is $4 for admission and skate rental. Victor and Carrie were only planning on spending $50 for the party. Will they have enough to pay for all the children to go skating?

15. Phyllis and Sidney are going to repaint their house this summer. There are 12 rooms altogether in their house. The painter charges $75 for each room. Phyllis and Sidney can only afford to pay $750 to repaint their house. Will this be enough to pay the painter to paint all 12 rooms?

Problem Solving with More Than One Operation

Part A

1. Frank is going to school today. He leaves home with $15 in his wallet. He spent $4 for lunch. On the way home he found $1 on the sidewalk. How much money should he have in his wallet when he gets home?

2. Gloria went to the supermarket to buy some fruit. She bought 6 apples and 8 oranges. After she got home, her son David ate 1 apple and 1 orange. How many pieces of fruit are left from the fruit Gloria bought at the supermarket?

3. Francis took his toy cars out to play in front of his house. He brought 8 cars and 4 trucks out with him. When he went in the house, he only found 9 cars and trucks. How many of his toys were missing?

4. Tyler has a collection of nickels and dimes that he has been saving. In his collection, there are 9 nickels and 10 dimes all from the 1930s. He went to a coin dealer to look at the coins for sale. He bought 4 more nickels and dimes from the 1930s. How many nickels and dimes from the 1930s does he have now?

5. Betty is 8 years older than her sister Charlotte. Charlotte is 5 years older than her sister Phyllis. If Betty is 26 years old, how old are her two sisters?

Part B

6. Mary went to the fabric store to purchase some lace. She had $20 in her purse when she left home. She bought 2 yards of lace at $3.50 per yard. She also found some buttons on sale for $1.99. Not including tax, how much did Mary spend and how much money should be left in her purse after she pays for her purchase?

7. Randy is a photographer. Last month he worked 3 weddings at $300 each and 2 children's parties at $150 each. How much did he make altogether for all 5 events.

8. Karen made brownies and cookies for a school bake sale. She charged 50¢ for each brownie and 25¢ for each cookie. She sold 20 brownies and 50 cookies. How much money did she raise for the bake sale?

9. Pedro drove 48 miles each way to visit his aunt and uncle. He spent $1.75 for each gallon of gas he used on this trip. He gets 16 miles from each gallon of gas. How much money did he spend on gas for the trip to visit his aunt and uncle?

10. Glen is buying new clothes for school. He spent $36 for each pair of jeans and $14 for each shirt he bought. He bought 4 pair of jeans and 6 shirts. Not including tax, how much did he spend on clothes?

Part C

11.. Alex and Esther have planned their summer trip. They will be going to Europe for four weeks. The round trip air fare to Europe is $575 per person. Their other costs average $750 for two per week. They also want to bring $75 spending money per person for each week. How much money will the entire trip cost for Alex and Esther?

12. Barney is taking his truck to his mechanic on Friday. He has been told that he should expect to pay the following: $175 for brakes, $135 for a tune-up, and $74 for each new tire. He needs 2 tires right now. The mechanic also charges $60 per hour for labor. It will take him 3 hours to do all the work. Barney must also pay 8% tax on everything except labor. How much should Barney expect to pay altogether?

13. Susan works for an insurance company. She earns $27.50 per

hour. Last week she worked 8 hours on Monday, Tuesday and Wednesday. On Thursday, she only worked 7 hours and she was ill on Friday. She went to work on Saturday for 4 hours to make up some of the time she lost on Friday. She did not work on Sunday. How much money did Susan earn for the entire week?

14. Donna is landscaping her front yard. At the nursery she bought 10 shrubs at $19 each and 2 fruit trees at $38 each. She also bought 3 flats of bedding plants to go around the shrubs and trees at $4 per flat. Find the total cost of plants not including tax.

15. Michael is putting ceramic tile on his kitchen floor. He needs 130 tiles at $2.25 per tile. He also needs 2 containers of grout at $15.75 per container and 2 containers of tile adhesive at $18.75 per container. He also needs a cement spreader at $6. He knows a contractor who will do the job for $300 including labor. Is it less expensive for him to do the job himself or should he hire the contractor for the job?

The real uses of math become more meaningful as you progress into the higher levels of math. The problems you have just worked on are truly the preliminary steps to a more increased awareness of the many uses of math. The importance of critical thinking becomes more and more evident as we pay closer attention to the most insignificant tasks that affect us daily.

The fact remains that problem solving had to begin somewhere. Perhaps it began with the basic bartering of goods. Maybe keeping simple records of things involved the most basic of concepts. What we do know is that we may never know how it really all began.

Mathematics is one of the most powerful tools we have at our disposal today. How we choose to use it is completely up to us. In the overall scheme of things, no matter what we do, we will never, ever get away from mathematics. It is just too much a part of our everyday lives. So the stronger our children become with their basic skills in problem solving, the more successful they are likely to become as adults.

Answers

Key Words

1.	more	2.	less	3. altogether	4.		more
5.	difference	6.	less than	7. total	8.		times
9.	divide	10.	in all				

Addition

1.	21 toys	2.	16 cards	3.	5 pairs	4.	4 ribbons
5.	15 crayons	6.	24 tools	7.	36 televisions	8.	13 items
9.	72 items	10.	72 CDs	11.	235 tiles	12.	640 square feet
13.	11,259 feet	14.	46 blocks	15.	12 items		

Subtraction

1.	3 coins	2.	3 baking sheets	3.	3 people	4.	2 dollars
5.	5 dollars	6.	23 bulbs	7.	168 bricks	8.	19 markers
9.	$139	10.	$11,160	11.	Jones Agency, $86	12.	$4,254
13.	76 quarts	14.	No, 9 pages	15.	590 feet		

Multiplication

1.	20 buttons	2.	54 hours	3.	$6 per hour	4.	36 letters
5.	70¢	6.	$208	7.	$9	8.	60 pages
9.	$15	10.	185 students	11.	52,800 miles	12.	$55,900
13.	1,260 miles	14.	$29.21	15.	715 miles		

Division

1.	3 animals	2.	4 slices	3.	4 books	4.	10 minutes
5.	5 minutes	6.	No	7.	$2.23	8.	18 students
9.	89¢	10.	79¢	11.	5 sites	12.	4 graduations
13.	21 beads	14.	Yes	15.	No		

More Than One Operation

1.	$12	2.	12 pieces	3.	3 toys
4.	23 coins	5.	Charlotte - 18 years, Phyllis - 13 years	6.	$8.99, $11.01
7.	$1,200	8.	$22.50	9.	$5.25
10.	$228	11.	$4,750	12.	$674.64
13.	$962.50	14.	$278		
15.	He should hire the contractor.				

Keep the Magic in Math

All authors share a common dream: Their books will be well-read and well-received and have an impact on the reader. We also share that vision for our book, but not only for you, the reader—the parent—but especially for your children. We hope that your child has not only learned the *skills* of doing math, but the *joy* of learning how to do it. There are, if you will pardon the mathematical pun, "dividends" your child can receive from discovering the magic in math, including heightened thinking skills, creativity, intellectual enthusiasm, and an overall confidence in dealing with numbers in particular and math in general. The point is to teach your child to enjoy math enough so that school mathematics or math discovered later in life will seem more natural and less intimidating. And who knows, maybe your child will grow up to be a mathematician, scientist, or engineer!

APPENDIX

1

Books on Math and Science for Adults

Abbott, Edwin. 1963. *Flatland.* New York: Barnes & Noble.
> A mathematical romp into the world of two dimensions through the eyes of a square.

Albers, Donald J., and G. L. Alexanderson (Eds.). 1985.
> *Mathematical People: Profiles and Interviews.* Chicago: Contemporary Books.
> Interviews and profiles of 25 of the world's greatest living mathematicians, how they work and live, and how they developed their love for mathematics.

Alic, Margaret. 1986. *Hypatia's Heritage: A History of Women in Science from Antiquity Through the Nineteenth Century.* Boston: Beacon Press.
> Hypatia was a brilliant mathematician in ancient Rome. But the fact that she was a woman makes her a relative unknown to most. Until now.

Anderson, Ronald, et al. 1970. *Developing Children's Thinking Through Science.* Englewood Cliffs, NJ: Prentice-Hall.

Bell, E. T. 1951. *Mathematics, Queen and Servant of Science.* New York: McGraw-Hill.
> Bell addresses the dual nature of mathematics, as both discovery and invention, a finding of and tool for science.

Bell, E. T. 1968. *Men of Mathematics.* New York: Simon & Schuster.
> The lives and achievements of the great mathematicians from Zeno to Poincare.

Brandes, Louis. 1979. *Science Can Be Fun.* Portland, ME: J. Weston Walch.

Bronowski, J. 1965. *Science and Human Values.* New York: Harper & Row.
A mathematician looks at the human side of science.

Bronowski, J. 1973. *The Ascent of Man.* Boston: Little, Brown & Co.
The book that accompanied the award-winning television show of the same name, which retraces the rise of civilization through the history of mathematics, science, and technology.

Burger, Dionys. 1965. *Sphereland.* New York: Barnes & Noble.
The sequel to Edwin Abbott's classic *Flatland,* Burger expands mathematical thinking through fictional characters into dimensions beyond belief.

Burke, James. 1978. *Connections.* Boston: Little, Brown & Co.
Television documentary producer looks at the unusual connections between math, science, technology, and society.

Burke, James. 1985. *The Day the Universe Changed.* Boston: Little, Brown & Co.
The 10 most important events in the history of science come alive in this companion to the television series of the same name.

Butts, David. 1975. *Children and Science: The Process of Teaching and Learning.* Englewood Cliffs, NJ: Prentice-Hall.

Cajori, Florian. 1961. *A History of Mathematicos.* New York: Macmillan.
A thorough history of mathematics by the man who translated Newton's great work, *Principia.*

Carin, Arthur, and Robert Sund. 1975. *Teaching Science Through Discovery.* Columbus: Charles E. Merrill Publishing Co.

Charles, R. I., and E. A. Silver (Eds.). 1988. *The Teaching and Assessing of Mathematical Problem Solving.* Reston, VA: National Council of Teachers of Mathematics.

Conners, Edward A. "A Decline in Mathematics Threatens Science—and the U.S." In *The Scientist,* 2:22 (November 28, 1988).

Davis, Philip J., and Reuben Hersh. 1986. *Descartes' Dream: The World According to Mathematics.* New York: Harcourt Brace Jovanovich.
An attempt to develop a heightened awareness of the relationships between humans and the mathematics they created through the ages, and how this system of mathematics has not only changed the world, but created our way of thinking.

Dethier, Vincent. 1962. *To Know a Fly.* New York: Holden-Day.
A biologist writes for the general public on the romance and reasons for being a scientist.

Epstein, Lewis. 1988. *Thinking Physics.* San Francisco: Insight Press.
An excellent "question and answer" approach to physics that is a great place for parents to find answers to children's questions. "Epstein's Law" is that "there is an easy way to explain anything."

Friedl, Alfred. 1972. *Teaching Science to Children: The Inquiry Approach Applied.* New York: Random House.

Gamow, George. 1961. *Puzzle-Math.* New York: Viking Press.

Ginsburg, H. P. 1977. *Children's Arithmetic: How They Learn It and How You Teach It.* New York: Van Nostrand Reinhold.

Gleick, James. 1987. *Chaos.* New York: Viking Press.
>   An award-winning, easy-to-read popularization of the new theory of chaos, the mathematics of order in a seemingly chaotic world.

Glenn, William H., and Donovan A. Johnson. 1961. *Exploring Mathematics on Your Own.* New York: Doubleday.
>   A good basic self-help book on mathematics.

Good, Ronald G. 1977. *How Children Learn Science.* New York: Macmillan.

Hardison, R. C. 1988. *Upon the Shoulders of Giants.* New York: University Press of America.
>   A highly readable, very stimulating history of the most important scientists and mathematicians in history.

Hawking, Stephen. 1988. *A Brief History of Time: From the Big Bang to Black Holes.* New York: Bantam Books.
>   A science classic in our time by the British astronomer and cosmologist who is revolutionizing our universal worldview.

Hellemans, Alexander, and Bryan Bunch. 1988. *The Timetables of Science.* New York: Simon & Schuster.
>   A chronology of the most important people and events in the history of science, technology, and mathematics.

Hubler, H. Clark. 1974. *Science for Children.* New York: Random House.

Huff, Darrell, and Irving Geis. 1954. *How to Lie with Statistics.* New York: W. W. Norton.

Huff, Darrell, and Irving Geis. 1959. *How to Take a Chance.* New York: W. W. Norton.
>   Huff and Geis's engaging and well-illustrated presentation makes statistics and probabilities not only easy to understand but actually fun!

Land, Frank. 1963. *The Language of Mathematics.* New York: Doubleday.
>   A classic that conveys the importance and beauty of mathematics.

Mason, J., L. Burton, and K. Stacey. 1982. *Thinking Mathematically.* Reading, MA: Addison-Wesley.

McCain, G., and E. M. Segal. 1969. *The Game of Science.* Monterey, CA: Brooks/Cole Publishing Co.
>   A good introduction to the basics of science that makes science fun.

Moore, Shirley. 1960. *Science Projects Handbook.* Washington, DC: Science Service.

Munson, Howard R. 1962. *Science Activities with Simple Things.* Belmont, CA: Fearon Pitman Publishers, Inc.

Olson, Richard. 1982. *Science Deified & Science Defied.* Berkeley: University of California Press.

    A thorough history of the development of mathematics and science through the ages.

Papert, Seymour. 1980. *Mindstorms: Children, Computers, and Powerful Ideas.* New York: Basic Books.

Pemberton, John E. 1963. *How to Find Out in Mathematics.* New York: Macmillan.

    A much more extensive guide to sources of mathematical information than is given in the appendices of this book. A good place to begin for further research on mathematics of any kind.

Peterson, Ivars. 1988. *Mathematical Tourist: Snapshots of Modern Mathematics.* New York: W. H. Freeman.

Prigogine, Ilya. 1984. *Order Out of Chaos: Man's New Dialogue with Nature.* New York: Bantam Books.

    One of the pioneering works on chaos theory by a pioneering mathematician, physicist, and Nobel prize winner, overturning our traditional ideas on the mechanical nature of the cosmos.

Sagan, Carl. 1979. *Broca's Brain.* New York: Random House.

    One of the world's most famous scientists shows the public the importance of math and science in our culture through this collection of essays.

Sagan, Carl. 1980. *Cosmos.* New York: Random House.

    The companion book to the most-watched documentary math and science series ever.

Sarton, George. 1936. *The Study of the History of Mathematics.* New York: Dover.

    An oldie but goodie, this classic by one of the founders of the mathematics and science history field lays the groundwork for generations interested in the history of mathematics.

Schoenfeld, A. H. 1985. *Mathematical Problem Solving.* New York: Academic Press.

Scott, John M. 1970. *The Everyday Living Approach to Teaching Elementary Science.* West Nyack, NY: Parker Publishing Co.

Shermer, M. B. 1989. *Teach Your Child Science.* Los Angeles: Lowell House/ Contemporary Books.

Stone, A. Harris, Fred Geis, and Louis Kuslan. 1971. *Experiences for Teaching Children Science.* Belmont, CA: Wadsworth Publishing.

Strongin, Herb. 1976. *Science on a Shoestring.* Reading, MA: Addison-Wesley.

Sund, Robert, William Tillery, and Leslie Trowbridge. 1975. *Investigate and Discover: Elementary Science Lessons.* Boston, MA: Allyn & Bacon, Inc.

Tammadge, Alan, and Phyllis Starr. 1977. *A Parents' Guide to School Mathematics.* School Mathematics Project Handbooks. Cambridge: Cambridge University Press.

Tanur, Judith. *Statistics: A Guide to the Unknown.* Florence, KY: Wadsworth Inc.

Trojack, Doris A. 1979. *Science with Children.* New York: McGraw-Hill.

UNESCO. 1962. *700 Science Experiments for Everyone.* Garden City, NY: Doubleday.

UNESCO. 1976. *New UNESCO Sourcebook for Science Teaching.* New York: UNIPUB, Inc.

Viorst, Judith. 1971. *150 Science Experiments Step-by-Step.* New York: Bantam Books.

Westfall, Richard S. 1980. *Never at Rest: A Biography of Isaac Newton.* Cambridge: Cambridge University Press.

The definitive biography of perhaps the most important and famous scientist and mathematician who ever lived, by an eminent historian of science.

APPENDIX

2

Books on Math and Science for Children
(With a little help from their parents)

Bendick, Jeanne. 1968. *Shapes.* New York: Franklin Watts.

Blackwelder, Sheila. 1980. *Science for All Seasons.* Englewood Cliffs, NJ: Prentice-Hall.

Science experiences and experiments for young children for every season of the year.

Charosh, M. 1971. *Rubber Bands, Baseballs and Doughnuts: A Book About Topology.* New York: Thomas Y. Crowell Co.

Charosh, M. 1971. *Straight Lines, Parallel Lines, Perpendicular Lines.* New York: Thomas Y. Crowell Co.

Cobb, Vicki, and Kathy Darling. 1980. *Bet You Can't! Science Impossibilities to Fool You.* New York: Lothrop, Lee & Shepard Books.

Dennis, J. R. 1971. *Fractions Are Parts of Things.* New York: Thomas Y. Crowell Co.

Froman, R. 1971. *Bigger and Smaller.* New York: Thomas Y. Crowell Co.

Gardner, Martin. 1981. *Entertaining Science Experiments with Everyday Objects.* New York: Dover.

Gardner, Robert. 1986. *Ideas for Science Projects.* New York: Franklin Watts.

A collection of simple and effective science experiments that parents and teachers can do with children.

Hays, Kim (Ed.). 1984. *T.V., Science and Kids: Teaching Our Children to Question.* New York: Addison-Wesley.
  A collection of essays by scientists and educators on using television productively.
Holt, Bess-Gene. 1977. *Science with Young Children.* Washington, DC: National Association for the Education of Young Children.
  An excellent resource for what every parent and teacher should know about math and science education for young children.
Holt, Michael. 1975. *Maps, Tracks, and the Bridges of Konigsberg.* New York: Thomas Y. Crowell Co.
Hurwitz, A., A. Goddard, and D. T. Epstein. 1975. *Number Games to Improve Your Child's Arithmetic.* New York: Funk & Wagnalls.
Lauber, Patricia. 1964. *The Story of Numbers.* New York: Random House.
Linn, C. F. 1971. *Estimation.* New York: Thomas Y. Crowell Co.
Loiry, William. 1983. *Winning with Science.* Loiry Publishing.
  A guide to science research, programs, and contests for students.
Medawar, Peter. 1979. *Advice to a Young Scientist.* New York: Harper & Row.
Milgrom, Harry. 1970. *ABC Science Experiments.* New York: Macmillan.
O'Brien, T. C. 1971. *Odds and Evens.* New York: Thomas Y. Crowell Co.
Razzell, A. G., and K. G. O. Watts. 1968. *Circles and Curves.* New York: Doubleday.
Rollins, W. E., and E. R. Ranucci. 1977. *Curiosities of the Cube.* New York: Thomas Y. Crowell Co.
Russell, S. P. 1970. *One, Two, Three and Many: A First Look at Numbers.* New York: Henry Z. Walck, Inc.
Schmidt, V. T., and V. N. Rockcastle. 1968. *Teaching Science with Everyday Things.* New York: McGraw-Hill.
Science for Beginners. 1965. Morristown: Silver Burdett.
Sitomer, Mindel and Harry. 1971. *Circles.* New York: Thomas Y. Crowell Co.
Srivastava, J. J. 1971. *Weighing and Balancing.* New York: Thomas Y. Crowell Co.
Trivett, Daphne H. 1974. *Shadow Geometry.* New York: Thomas Y. Crowell Co.
Whitney, D. C. 1970. *The Easy Book of Division.* New York: Franklin Watts.
Wood, Elizabeth. 1975. *Science from Your Airplane Window.* New York: Dover.

APPENDIX

3

Math and Science Periodicals for Parents and Children

Appraisal: Science Books for Young Children. Three issues per year. Children's Science Book Review Committee, 36 Cummington St., Boston, MA 02215. Reviews of science books for children.

Chickadee. Ten issues per year. Young Naturalist Foundation, P.O. Box 11314, Des Moines, IA 50304.
Information about and activities involving nature for children.

Discover: The Newsmagazine of Science. Monthly. Time-Life Books, Time-Life Building, 541 N. Fairbanks Court, Chicago, IL 60611.
An illustrated magazine of popularized science for the general public.

Electric Company. Ten issues per year. Children's Television Workshop, One Lincoln Plaza, New York, NY 10023.
A thematic approach gives children different activities each month to explore.

Odyssey: Young People's Magazine of Astronomy and Outer Space. Monthly. Astromedia Corporation, 625 E. St. Paul Ave., Milwaukee, WI 53202.
Science, space, and astronomy, well illustrated for children.

Owl. Ten issues per year. Young Naturalist Foundation, P.O. Box 11314, Des Moines, IA 50304.
A magazine for children's inquiring minds about science and nature. Develops wonder, and a thirst for more.

Science and Children. Eight issues per year. National Science Teachers Association, 1742 Connecticut Ave., N.W., Washington, DC 20009.

Illustrated science ideas for elementary and junior high school science teachers.

Science Weekly. Eighteen issues per year. Science Weekly, P.O. Box 70154, Washington, DC 20088-0154.

A thematic approach; each issue deals with a specific topic in science, math, or technology, with teaching notes for parents, including a bibliography for further exploration of a topic, questions to ask your child about that science subject, and hands-on activities for learning about a particular science.

Scienceland. Eight issues per year. Scienceland, Inc., 501 Fifth Ave., New York, NY 10017-6165.

Color photographs and excellent illustrations bring to life the world of science and nature for your child. Each issue focuses on a particular subject such as math, space, stars.

3-2-1 Contact. Ten issues per year. Children's Television Workshop, P.O. Box 2933, Boulder, CO 80321.

Science magazine for children based on the TV series.

APPENDIX

4

Math Careers for Your Child

A legitimate question any child or adolescent may ask about learning math is, "Why?"

"Why should I learn math?" he or she may ask. It may be more motivating for you, the parent, if you know that in addition to the fun of playing with numbers and shapes, as we've been doing in this book, there is a very practical side to learning math. It will open up your child's future to careers not possible without it.

The statistics on the education crisis, which we cited at the beginning of this book, foretell a future that makes math and science students extremely valuable. This not only translates into prestige and honor but into financial security as well. The free-market principle of supply and demand is hard at work here. All the demographics point to a future that requires more math and science majors than there are students applying for such positions in our colleges. One way to give your child a giant head start is to generate an interest in math by making it fun. The interest in college and jobs will come later.

Though it may not seem like it at first blush, a college undergraduate degree in math can do wonders. Your child can take one of two possible routes with a degree in mathematics: (1) continue his or her education in a university graduate program, or (2) begin a working career. The first part of this appendix lists some of the academic departments attracting math majors; the second part lists some of the jobs attracting math majors.

Graduate Academic Departments Attracting Math Majors

Applied Mathematics

Applied Sciences

Astronomy

Biostatistics

Business

Chemistry

Cognitive Science

Computer Science

Economics

Electrical Engineering

Engineering–Economic Systems

Epidemiology

Industrial Engineering

Law

Management and Information Systems

Mathematical Sciences

Mathematics

Medicine

Operations Research

Physics

Policy Planning

Psychology

Public Health Sciences

Public Policy and Management

Statistics

Theoretical and Applied Mechanics

Careers Attracting Math Majors

The following list was compiled by the Marketing Department of the publishing company Scott, Foresman/Little, Brown. In a survey, college and university professors were asked what their graduates were doing with their degrees in math. The positions alphabetically listed below are actually held by individuals with undergraduate and graduate degrees in mathematics.

Accountant

Actuary

Aerospace Engineer

Air Traffic Controller

Aircraft Design Engineer

Airline Navigator

Architect

Artificial Intelligence Group Analyst

Astronaut

Astronomer

Auditor

Automotive Engineer

Bank Teller

Banker
Biologist
Biomedical Engineer
Biometrician
Biostatistician
Bookkeeper
Broadcast Technician
Business Administrator
Business Machine Operator
CAD/CAM (Computer-Aided Design/Computer-Aided Manufacturing) Engineer
Cartographer
Certified Public Accountant
Chemical Process Technician
Chemical Research Projects Leader
Chemist
Civil Engineer
Commercial Pilot
Community College Instructor
Computational Physicist
Computer Consultant
Computer Engineer
Computer Graphics Programmer
Computer Programmer
Computer Scientist
Computer Security Analyst
Computer Systems Analyst
Construction Engineer
Contractor
Cost Estimator
Credit Analyst
Credit Representative
Data Control Coordinator

Data Processing Analyst
Data Processing Consultant
Data Processor
Demographer
Design Engineer
Econometrician
Economist
Electrical Engineer
Engineering Specialist
Engineering Technician Optician
Estimator
Financial Analyst
Financial Services Representative
Flight Engineer
Food Scientist
Geodesist
Geographer
Geologist
Geophysicist
High School Principal
Industrial Engineer
Industrial Purchasing Agent
Industrial Traffic Manager
Information Analyst
Instrument Maker
Laboratory Supervisor
Land Operations Manager
Loan Management Officer
Maintenance Director
Manager of Computer Services
Market Research Analyst
Marketing Manager
Materials and Systems Manager
Mathematical Economist

Mathematician

Mechanical Engineer

Meteorological Technician

Meteorologist

Musicologist

Navigator

Nuclear Scientist

Numerical Analyst

Oceanographer

Operations Research Analyst

Optometrist

Orthopedic Surgeon

Payroll Specialist

Pension Fund Analyst

Philosopher

Physician

Physicist

Post-Doctoral Research Associate

Psychologist

Psychometrician

Product Testing Engineering Manager

Quality Assurance Specialist

Rate Analyst

Reliability Engineer

Research Administrator

Research Assistant

Safety Engineer

Secondary School Teacher

Seismologist

Senior Budget Analyst

Senior Energy Auditor

Software Design Engineer

Software Specialist

Space Guidance Manager

Statistician

Stockbroker

Strategic Planner

Surveyor

Systems Analyst

Systems Engineer

Systems Support Supervisor

Tax Consultant

Technical Writer

Telecommunications Analyst

Teletraffic Analyst

Test Engineer

Transportation Operations Manager

Treasurer/Financial Officer

Underwriter

University Professor

Weapon Systems Analyst

Where to Get Information About Careers in Mathematics

The Mathematical Association of America (MAA) collects and publishes information on careers in mathematics, and can be reached at 1529 Eighteenth St., N.W., Washington, DC 20036.

For further information about careers in mathematics, see the following books and brochures that can be obtained by writing the addresses given:

A Profile of the Woman Engineer. Society of Women Engineers, 345 E. 47th St., New York, NY 10017.

Actuary. Careers, P.O. Box 135, Largo, FL 33540.

Careers for Women in Mathematics. Association for Women in Mathematics, P.O. Box 178, Wellesley College, Wellesley, MA 02181.

Careers in Applied Mathematics. Society for Industrial and Applied Mathematics, 117 S. 17th St., Philadelphia, PA 19103.

Career Mathematics: Industry and the Trades. Houghton Mifflin Co., One Beacon St., Boston, MA 02108.

Careers in Mathematics. American Mathematical Society, P.O. Box 6248, Providence, RI 02940.

Careers in Operations Research and the Educational Programs in Operations Research/Management Science. Operations Research Society of America, Mount Royal & Guilford Avenues, Baltimore, MD 21201.

Careers in Statistics. American Statistical Association, 806 15th St., N.W., Washington, DC 20005.

Employment Outlook for Computer and Mathematics Related Occupations. Superintendent of Documents, U.S. Government Printing Office, Washington, DC 20402.

Mathematician. Careers, P.O. Box 135, Largo, FL 33540.

Opportunities in Science and Engineering. A Chartbook Presentation, Second Edition. Commission on Professionals in Science and Technology, 1500 Massachusetts Ave., N.W., Suite 831, Washington, DC 20005.

Physics in Your Future. American Physical Society, Committee on the Status of Women in Physics, 335 E. 45th St., New York, NY 10017.

Profiles in Applied Mathematics. Society for Industrial and Applied Mathematics, 117 S. 17th St., Philadelphia, PA 19103.

Programmer. Careers, P.O. Box 135, Largo, FL 33540.

Science Career Exploration for Women. National Science Teachers Association, 1742 Connecticut Ave., N.W., Washington, DC 20009.

Science Education for You? National Science Teachers Association, 1742 Connecticut Ave., N.W., Washington, DC 20009.

Statistician. Careers, P.O. Box 135, Largo, FL 33540.

Statistics as a Career: Women at Work. American Statistical Association, Committee on Women in Statistics, 806 15th St., N.W., Washington, DC 20005.

Systems Analyst. Careers, P.O. Box 135, Largo, FL 33540.

The Actuarial Profession. Society of Actuaries, 500 Park Blvd., Itasca, IL 60143.

The Chronicle Mathematics and Science Occupations Guidebook. Chronicle Guidance Publications, Inc., P.O. Box 1190, Moravia, NY 11318.

The Technological Marketplace: Supply and Demand for Scientists and Engineers. Commission on Professionals in Science and Technology, 1500 Massachusetts Ave., N.W., Washington, DC 20005.

Women Scientists Roster. National Science Teachers Association, 1742 Connecticut Ave., N.W., Washington, DC 20009.

APPENDIX

5

Math, Science, and Technology Museums by Region and State

Southwest

(Arizona, California, Colorado, Hawaii, New Mexico, Utah)

Arizona

Arizona Museum of Science and Technology
80 N. Second St., Phoenix, AZ 85004; 602/256-9388.

Center for Meteorite Studies
Arizona State University, Tempe, AZ 85187; 602/965-6511.

Tucson Children's Museum
300 E. University Blvd., Tucson, AZ 85705; 602/884-7511.

California

Bowers Museum
2002 N. Main St., Santa Ana, CA 92706; 714/972-1900.

California Academy of Science
Golden Gate Park, San Francisco, CA 94118; 415/221-5100.

California Museum of Science and Industry
700 State Dr., Los Angeles, CA 90037; 213/744-7400.

Diablo Valley College Museum
Golf Club Rd., Pleasant Hills, CA 94523; 415/685-1230.

The Discovery Center
1944 N. Winery Ave., Fresno, CA 93703; 209/251-5533.

The Exploratorium
3601 Lyon St., San Francisco, CA 94123; 415/563-7337.

Griffith Park Observatory
2800 E. Observatory Rd., Los Angeles, CA 90028; 213/664-1191.

Lawrence Hall of Science
University of California, Berkeley, CA 94720; 415/642-5133.

Reuben H. Fleet Space Theater and Science Center
1875 El Prado, Balboa Park, San Diego, CA 92103; 619/238-1233.

Sacramento Science Center and Junior Museum
3615 Auburn Blvd., Sacramento, CA 95821; 916/449-8255.

Colorado

Denver Museum of Natural History/ The Hall of Life
2001 Colorado Blvd., Denver, CO 80206; 719/376-6423.

Hawaii

The Bishop Museum
1525 Bernice St., Honolulu, HI 96817; 808/847-3511.

New Mexico

Musuem of New Mexico
113 Lincoln Ave., Santa Fe, NM 87503; 505/827-6450.

Utah

Children's Museum of Utah
840 N. 300 West, Salt Lake City, UT 84103; 801/328-3383.

Hansen Planetarium
15 S. State St., Salt Lake City, UT 84111; 801/538-2104.

Northwest

(Oregon, Washington)

Oregon

Oregon Museum of Science and Industry
4015 S.W. Canyon Rd., Portland, OR 97221; 503/222-2828.

Willamette Science and Technology Center
2300 Centennial Blvd., Eugene, OR 97440; 206/325-4510.

Washington

Hanford Science Center
825 Jadwin Ave., Box 1970, Mail Stop A1-60, Richland, WA 99352; 509/376-6374.

Pacific Science Center
200 Second Ave. N., Seattle, WA 98109; 206/443-2001.

Midwest

(Illinois, Indiana, Michigan, Ohio, Wisconsin)

Illinois

Lakeview Museum of the Arts and Sciences
1125 W. Lake Ave., Peoria, IL 61614; 309/686-7000.

Museum of Science and Industry
57th & Lake Shore Dr., Chicago, IL 60637; 312/684-1414.

Museum of the Chicago Academy of Sciences
2001 N. Clark St., Chicago, IL 60614; 312/549-0606.

Indiana

The Children's Museum, Indianapolis
P.O. Box 3000, Indianapolis, IN 46206; 317/924-5431.

Evansville Museum of Arts and Sciences
411 S.E. Riverside Dr., Evansville, IN 47713; 812/425-2406.

Michigan

Children's Museum, Detroit Public Schools
67 E. Kirby, Detroit, MI 48202; 313/494-1210.

Cranbrook Institute of Science
500 Lone Pine Rd., Bloomfield Hills, MI 48013; 313/645-3261.

Detroit Science Center
5020 John R. St., Detroit, MI 48202; 313/577-8400.

Impression 5 Science Museum
200 Museum Dr., Lansing, MI 48933; 517/485-8116.

Michigan Space Center
2111 Emmons Rd., Jackson, MI 49201; 517/787-4425.

The Michigan State University Museum
West Circle Dr., East Lansing, MI 48824; 517/355-2370.

Ohio

Cleveland Children's Museum
10730 Euclid Ave., Cleveland, OH 44106; 216/791-7114.

Cleveland Health Education Museum
8911 Euclid Ave., Cleveland, OH 44106; 216/231-5010.

Ohio's Center of Science and Industry
280 E. Broad St., Columbus, OH 43215; 614/228-5619.

Wisconsin

Discovery World Museum of Science, Economics and Technology
818 W. Wisconsin Ave., Milwaukee, WI 53233; 414/765-9966.

Milwaukee Public Museum
800 W. Wells St., Milwaukee, WI 53233; 414/278-2700.

North Central

(Iowa, Kansas, Minnesota, Missouri, Nebraska)

Iowa

The Science Center of Iowa
4500 Grand Ave., Des Moines, IA 50312; 515/274-4138.

Kansas

Kansas Learning Center for Health
309 Main St., Halstead, KS 67056; 316/835-2662.

Minnesota

The Mayo Medical Museum
Mayo Clinic, 200 First St., S.W., Rochester, MN 55901; 507/284-3280.

Science Museum of Minnesota
30 E. 10th St., St. Paul, MN 55101; 612/221-9410.

Missouri

The Kansas City Museum
3218 Gladstone Blvd., Kansas City, MO 64123; 816/483-8300.

The Magic House, St. Louis's Children Museum
516 S. Kirkwood Rd., St. Louis, MO 63122; 314/822-8900.

St. Louis Science Center and Science Park
Forest Park, 5050 Oakland Ave., St. Louis, MO 63110; 314/289-4400.

Nebraska

University of Nebraska State Museum of Natural Science
212 Morrill Hall, 14th & U Sts., Lincoln, NE 68588; 402/472-2637.

South Central

(Arkansas, Louisiana, Oklahoma, Texas)

Arkansas

Arkansas Museum of Science and History
MacArthur Park, Little Rock, AR 72202; 501/371-3521.

Louisiana

Louisiana Nature and Science Center
11000 Lake Forest Blvd., New Orleans, LA 70127; 504/241-9606.

LSU Museum of Geoscience
Howe-Russell Geoscience Complex, Room 135, Louisiana State University, Baton Rouge, LA 70803; 504/388-2296.

Oklahoma

Kirkpatrick Center Museum Complex
2100 N.E. 52nd St., Oklahoma City, OK 73111; 405/427-5461.

Omniplex Science Museum
2100 N.E. 52nd St., Oklahoma City, OK 73111; 405/424-5545.

Texas

Don Harrington Discovery Center
1200 Streit Dr., Amarillo, TX 79106; 806/255-9547.

Fort Worth Museum of Science and History
1501 Montgomery St., Ft. Worth, TX 76107; 817/732-1631.

Houston Museum of Medical Science
1 Herman Circle Dr., Houston, TX 77030; 713/529-3766.

Insights—El Paso Science Museum
303 N. Oregon St., El Paso, TX 79901; 915/542-2990.

The Science Place
P.O. Box 11158, Fair Park, Dallas, TX 75223; 214/428-7200.

Strecker Museum
South 4th St., Baylor University, Waco, TX 76798; 817/755-1110.

Northeast

(Connecticut, Maryland, Massachusetts, New Jersey, New York, Pennsylvania, Vermont)

Connecticut

Lutz Children's Museum
247 S. Main St., Manchester, CT 06040; 203/643-0949.

Museum of Art, Science, and Industry
4450 Park Ave., Bridgeport, CT 06604; 203/372-3521.

Science Museum of Connecticut
950 Trout Brook Dr., West Hartford, CT 06119; 203/236-2961.

Thames Science Center
Gallows Lane, New London, CT 06320; 203/442-0391.

Maryland

Howard B. Owens Science Center
9601 Greenbelt Rd., Lanham, MD 20706; 301/577-8718.

Maryland Academy of Sciences/Maryland Science Center
601 Light St., Baltimore, MD 21230; 301/685-2370.

Massachusetts

The Children's Museum
Museum Wharf, 300 Congress Ave., Boston, MA 02210; 617/426-6500.

The Computer Museum
Museum Wharf, 300 Congress Ave., Boston, MA 02210; 617/426-2800.

The Harvard University Museums
24 Oxford St., Cambridge, MA 02138; 617/495-1000.

Museum of Science, Boston
Science Park, Boston, MA 02114; 617/589-0100.

Springfield Science Museum
236 State St., Springfield, MA 01103; 413/733-1194.

New Jersey

Monmouth Museum
Newman Springs Rd., P.O. Box 359, Lincroft, NJ 07738; 201/747-2266.

Space Studies Institute
P.O. Box 82, Princeton, NJ 08540; 609/921-0377.

New York

American Museum of Natural History/Hayden Planetarium
Central Park West at 79th St., New York, NY 10024; 212/769-5000.

Brookhaven National Laboratory, Exhibit Center—Science Museum
Upton, NY 11973; 516/282-4049.

Buffalo Museum of Science
Humboldt Pkwy., Buffalo, NY 14211; 716/896-5200.

Discovery Center of Science & Technology
321 S. Clinton St., Syracuse, NY 13202; 315/425-9068.

Museum of Holography
11 Mercer St., New York, NY 10013; 212/925-0581.

New York Hall of Science
P.O. Box 1032, 47-01 111th St., Corona, NY 11368; 718/699-0005.

Robertson Center for the Arts and Sciences
30 Front St., Binghamton, NY 13905; 607/772-0660.

Schenectady Museum
2500 W. Broad St., Schenectady, NY 12308; 804/367-1013.

Science Museum of Long Island
1526 N. Plandome Rd., Manhasset, NY 11030; 516/627-9400.

Pennsylvania

The Academy of Natural Sciences of Philadelphia
19th & Benjamin Franklin Pkwy., Philadelphia, PA 19103; 215/299-1100.

Buhl Science Center
Allegheny Square, Pittsburgh, PA 15212; 412/321-4302.

Franklin Institute Science Museum and Planetarium and the Museum-to-Go Resource Center
20th and Benjamin Franklin Pkwy., Philadelphia, PA 19103; 215/488-1200.

Vermont

Fairbanks Museum and Planetarium
Main & Prospect Sts., St. Johnsbury, VT 05819; 802/748-2372.

Southeast

(Alabama, Florida, Georgia, Kentucky, Mississippi, North Carolina, South Carolina, Tennessee, Virginia)

Alabama

The Discovery Place
1320 33rd St. South, Birmingham, AL 35205; 205/939-1176.

Red Mountain Museum
1421 22nd St. South, Birmingham, AL 35205; 205/933-4152.

Florida

The Discovery Center
231 S.W. 2nd Ave., Ft. Lauderdale, FL 33301; 305/462-4116.

John Young Museum and Planetarium, Orlando Science Center
810 E. Rollins St., Orlando, FL 32803; 305/896-7151.

Museum of Arts and Science
1040 Museum Blvd., Daytona Beach, FL 32014; 904/255-0285.

Museum of Science and Industry
4801 E. Fowler Ave., Tampa, FL 33617; 813/985-5531.

Museum of Science and Space Transit Planetarium
3280 S. Miami Ave., Miami, FL 33129; 305/854-4247.

The South Florida Science Museum
4801 Dreher Trail N., West Palm Beach, FL 33405; 305/832-2026.

Georgia

Fernbank Science Center
156 Heaton Park Dr., N.E., Atlanta, GA 30307; 404/378-4311.

Museum of Arts and Sciences
4182 Forsyth Rd., Macon, GA 31210; 912/477-3232.

Kentucky

The Living Arts and Science Center, Inc.
362 Walnut St., Lexington, KY 40508; 606/252-5222.

Museum of History and Science
727 W. Main St., Louisville, KY 40202; 502/589-4584.

Mississippi

Gulf Coast Research Laboratory, J. L. Scott Marine Education Center
P.O. Box 7000, Ocean Springs, MS 39564; 601/374-5550.

Mississippi Museum of Natural Science
111 N. Jefferson St., Jackson, MS 39202; 601/354-7303.

North Carolina

Nature Science Center
Museum Dr., Winston-Salem, NC 27105; 919/767-6730.

North Carolina Museum of Life and Science
433 Murray Ave., Durham, NC 27704; 919/477-0431.

Science Museums of Charlotte, Inc./Nature Museum/Discovery Place
301 N. Tryon St., Charlotte, NC 29202; 704/372-6262.

South Carolina

The Charleston Museum
360 Meeting St., Charleston, SC 29403; 803/722-2996.

Roper Mountain Science Center
504 Roper Mountain Rd., Greenville, SC 29615; 803/297-0232.

Tennessee

American Museum of Science & Energy
300 S. Tulane Ave., Oak Ridge, TN 37830; 615/576-3200.

Cumberland Science Museum
800 Ridley Rd., Nashville, TN 37203; 615/259-6099.

Memphis Pink Palace Museum and Planetarium
3050 Central Ave., Memphis, TN 38111; 901/454-5603.

Virginia

Science Museum of Virginia
2500 W. Broad Ave., Richmond, VA 23220; 804/257-1013.

Science Museum of Western Virginia
1 Market Square, Roanoke, VA 24011; 703/343-7876.

Virginia Living Museum
524 J. Clyde Morris Blvd., Newport News, VA 23601; 804/595-1900.

District of Columbia

Capital Children's Museum
800 Third St., N.E., Washington, DC 20002; 202/543-8600.

Explorers Hall
17th and M Sts., N.W., Washington, DC 20036; 202/857-7000.

National Air and Space Museum
Independence Ave. & 7th St., Washington, DC 20560; 202/357-1504.

National Museum of American History
(Includes Math, Science, and Technology)
12th St. & Constitution Ave., N.W., Washington, DC 20560; 202/357-1300.

Canada

National Museum of Science and Technology
1867 St. Laurent Blvd., Ottawa Terminal, Ottawa, Ontario, K1G-5A3;
613/991-3044.

Ontario Science Centre
770 Don Mills Rd., Don Mills, Ontario, M3C 1T3; 416/429-4100.

APPENDIX

6

Scientific Companies That Publish Math and Science Catalogues and Distribute Teaching Tools

The following scientific companies can be contacted by mail to find out what they offer in the way of teaching tools to teach children science. Most have catalogues, newsletters, charts and posters, and other such *free* items that they would be happy to send you and your child.

Accent! Science
301 Cass St., Saginaw, MI 48602.
    Astronomical and earth science models for elementary age kids.

Activity Resources Co., Inc.
P.O. Box 4875, Hayward, CA 94540.
    Chemistry materials.

Aims Education Foundation
P.O. Box 7766, Fresno, CA 93747.
    Science and math activity books.

Bausch and Lomb
1400 N. Goodman St., Rochester, NY 14602.
    Microscopes for children.

CEBCO
9 Kulick Rd., Fairfield, NJ 07006.
   Science books and related materials.

Central Scientific Co. (CENCO)
2600 Kostner Ave., Chicago, IL 60623.
   Science materials and equipment.

Continental Press
Elizabethtown, PA 17022.
   Electricity experiments, science booklets.

Creative Learning Press
P.O. Box 320, Mansfield Center, CT 06250.
   Science and general education books and materials.

Creative Learning Systems, Inc.
9889 Hilbret St., Suite E, San Diego, CA 92131.
   Materials and equipment for science and technology.

Creative Publications, Inc.
P.O. Box 238, Palo Alto, CA 94302.
   Catalog of creative math and science manipulative materials.

Cuisenaire Company of America, Inc.
12 Church St., New Rochelle, NY 10802.
   Science and mathematics activity books.

Edmund Scientific Co.
7789 Edscorp Building, Barrington, NJ 08007.
   Astronomy materials including star charts, planet finders, prisms, and free
   issues of *Astronomy News.*

Energy Learning Center/Edison Electric Institute
1111 19th St., N.W., Washington, DC 20036.
   Films and science learning kits for information on energy.

Energy Sciences, Inc.
16728 Oakmont Ave., Gaithersburg, MD 20877.
   Energy toys and solar-powered kits.

Estes Industries
P.O. Box 227, Penrose, CO 81240.
   Information on model rocketry, materials needed, how to build a rocket,
   how to build a wind tunnel, and more.

Fisher Scientific Co.
4901 W. Lemoyne, Chicago, IL 60651.
   Information on education and science materials.

Forestry Suppliers, Inc.
205 W. Rankin St., Jackson, MS 39204.
  Biology, geology, and environmental hands-on tools and kits.

Frey Scientific
905 Hickory Ln., Mansfield, OH 44905.
  Astronomy, physics, chemistry, and geology equipment and supplies.

Hubbard Scientific Co.
1946 Raymond Dr., Northbrook, IL 60062.
  Science media and materials.

Lab-Aids, Inc.
130 Wilbur Place, Bohemia, NY 11716.
  General science equipment and materials.

Learning Things, Inc.
68A Broadway, P.O. Box 436, Arlington, MA 02174.
  Books, supplies, and lab equipment.

LEGO Systems, Inc.
555 Taylor Rd., Enfield, CT 06082.
  Manipulative toys to teach physical science.

NASA
400 Maryland Ave., S.W., Washington, DC
  Space Shuttle information; what it takes to be an astronaut.

OHAUS
29 Hanover Rd., Florham Park, NJ 07932.
  Mathematical and science equipment.

Play-Jour, Inc.
200 Fifth Ave., Suite 1024, New York, NY 10010.
  Write for the Capsela Scientific Kit with 25 lessons on the physical sciences.

Sargent-Welch Scientific Co.
7300 N. Linder Ave., Skokie, IL 60077.
  Science materials.

Savi/Selph, Center for Multisensory Learning
Lawrence Hall of Science, University of California, Berkeley, CA 94720.
  Science activities for handicapped children.

Science Kit, Inc.
Lonowanda, NY 14150.
  General science materials and equipment.

Science Man
P.O. Box 56036, Harwood Heights, IL 60656.
   Science resource books.

Science Research Associates, Inc.
259 E. Erie St., Chicago, IL 60611.
   "Inquiry Development Program" materials and films.

Science Service
1719 North St., N.W., Washington, DC
   Small kits of science materials for all sciences.

Tops Learning Systems
10978 S. Mulino Rd., Canby, OR 97013.
   Math and science information and materials that are inexpensive.

Toys 'n' Things
906 N. Dale, St. Paul, MN 55103
   Publishes *Teachables from Trashables: Homemade Toys That Teach.*

Index

addition, defined, 54
addition games, 54–86
additive nature of numbers, 111
Alice's Adventures in Wonderland, 9–10

Carroll, Lewis, 9, 24
Committee on the Mathematical
    Sciences in the Year 2000, 3
commutative property of
    multiplication, 110
comparing, 26
comparing games, 26–33
counting, 35
counting games, 42–53

dividing with pigs and pens, 131–136
division defined, 129
division games, 129–145
division, long, 137–144
Dodgson, Charles Lutwidge, 9–10

Escalante, Jaime, 4

Feelies game, 28–29
Feynman, Richard, 16

Galileo, 16

Helping Mommy and Daddy
    game, 32–33
How High Can You Count? game, 50
"How Many" and "How Much"
    game, 43
How Many Are There? game, 47

Kumon Mathamatex, 4
Kumon, Toru, 4

Let's Count to Ten game, 45
Let's Measure Cookies game, 40–41

math, the magic of, 146
math on paper, 79–86
Mathematical Sciences Education
    Board, 2
mathematics, defined, 15

measuring, 35
measuring games, 40–42
Mixing and Matching game, 48
Much Ado About Nothing, 113
multiplication defined, 107
multiplication games, 128
multiplication table, 116
multiplication with coins, 122–126
multiplication with pigs, pens, and
     pundreds, 119–121
multiplicative nature of numbers, 111
Multiplying Fun game, 115–117

naming, 25–26
naming games, 26–33
National Institute for Education
     Research, 4
National Research Council, 2
Number Table, 53

Onesies and Twosies game, 44
ordering, 34
ordering games, 35–40

Pennies, Dimes, and Dollars
     game, 103–105
Pigs, Pens, and Pundreds, 58–73

Pigs in a Pen Again game, 83–91
Playing the Numbers game, 55
Pundreds of Pigs, 74–79

Shapies game, 29–31
sorting, 26
sorting games, 26–33
Spoons game, 28
subtraction, defined, 87
subtraction games, 87–105

The Answer Game, 117
The Back and Forth Game, 117–118
The Bead Game, 39
The Counting Game, 51
The Squares Game, 112–113
There's Nothing to It! game, 91
Through the Looking-Glass, 9–10, 24
Turning the Tables game, 114–115

What Did You Do When You Woke Up?
     game, 38
What is It? game, 28
What Kind of Measure is It?
     game, 41–42
Which Came First? game, 36–38
Why is a Dog a Dog? game, 27–28

About the Authors

ARTHUR BENJAMIN, PH.D.

Arthur Benjamin earned a B.S. in applied mathematics at Carnegie-Mellon University, and an M.S.E. and Ph.D. at Johns Hopkins University. He is currently assistant professor of mathematics at Harvey Mudd College in Claremont, California. His mathematical research focuses on combinatorics and operations research, areas of applied mathematics.

Dr. Benjamin has also performed for years as a magician and is included in James ("The Amazing") Randi's latest book on magic for his unique skills as a "mathemagician." He has also worked with memory experts on memory strategies and their application in improving math skills. Since 1982 Dr. Benjamin has been astounding audiences throughout the United States with his numerical magic, which he calls "mathemagics." He has also appeared on numerous talk shows on radio and television and has been featured in Steven B. Smith's *The Great Mental Calculators* as the only living American "calculating prodigy." He combines his talents in magic, memory, and his years of training and experience as a mathematician with public performances of "lightning calculations," in which he multiplies 2-, 3-, and even 4-digit numbers faster than an individual with a calculator. To further his claim that almost anyone can master his system, Dr. Benjamin is currently working on educational material that outline his "mathemagics" program.

MICHAEL BRANT SHERMER, PH.D.

Michael Shermer received a Ph.D. in history from Claremont Graduate School, an M.A. in experimental psychology from the California State University, Fullerton, and a B.A. in psychology from Pepperdine University. He teaches the history of science, technology, and culture in the Cultural Studies Program at Occidental College in Los Angeles.

He is the publisher of *Skeptic* magazine, the director of the Skeptics Society, and the organizer and host of the Skeptics Lecture Series at the California Institute of Technology (Caltech). He is the author of *Why People Believe Weird Things, Teach Your Child Science,* and coauthor of *Mathemagics* with Arthur Benjamin. Dr. Shermer has just finished a biography of the nineteenth century co-discoverer of natural selection, Alfred Russel Wallace, titled *Heretic-Scientist,* and is presently working on *The Chaos of History* applying chaos and complexity theory, feedback loops, and complex adaptive systems to human history. He has several published papers in this field in noted scientific and historical journals, and writes a regular column for *Skeptic* on a wide range of controversial issues in science and history.

Dr. Shermer has also written numerous cycling books based on a ten-year professional career as an ultra-marathon cyclist and competitor in the 3,000-mile, nonstop transcontinental Race Across America, and has been featured numerous times on ABC's *Wide World of Sports* and ESPN.